Theory Test for Motorcyclists

The **official questions** and **answers** for **learner riders**

Get 10% off marked prices*
On AA Road Atlases
and Street by Street

Simply visit **theAA.com/shop** and enter the promo code **DRIVERS1** at the checkout to claim your discount, terms and conditions apply.

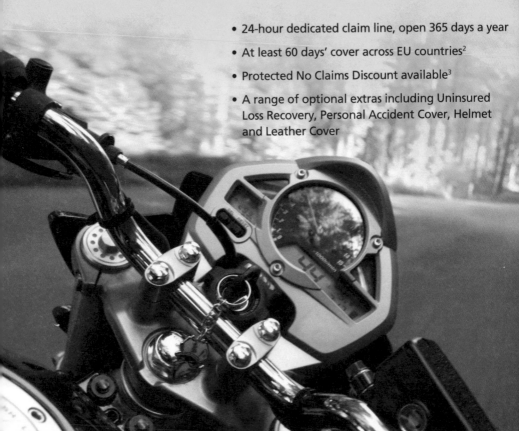

Cover from £85 with AA Motorcycle Insurance

At the AA we think good value is important. That's why we can offer you Motorcycle Insurance from just £85. Just give us a call and we'll compare prices from our panel of leading insurers to get you the best deal we can.

- 24-hour dedicated claim line, open 365 days a year
- At least 60 days' cover across EU countries[2]
- Protected No Claims Discount available[3]
- A range of optional extras including Uninsured Loss Recovery, Personal Accident Cover, Helmet and Leather Cover

Call 0800 107 9785

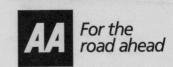

For the road ahead

Opening hours: Monday-Friday 8.30am-7.00pm, Saturdays 8.30am-3.00pm, Sundays & Bank Holidays 10.00am-2.00pm

You may contact us using Text Relay. Information is also available in large print, Braille and Audio on request. Please call for details.

Produced by AA Publishing.

ISBN: 978-0-7495-6729-3

Published by AA Publishing (a trading name of AA Media Limited, whose registered
office is Fanum House, Basing View, Basingstoke, Hampshire RG21 4EA; registered
number 06112600).

Visit AA Publishing at theAA.com/shop

Colour separation by Keene Group, Andover
Printed and bound by G. Canale & C. s.p.a., Torino, Italy

Image credits
Front cover: © fckncg/Alamy
Back cover: © Oleksiy Maksymenko/Alamy

A04483

While every effort has been made to include the
widest possible range of questions available at the
time of printing, the Government may from time
to time change, add or remove questions, and the
publisher cannot be held responsible for questions
that may appear on a Theory Test which were not
available for inclusion in this book.

Contents

Introduction

About the test

You want to pass your bike test and take advantage of the freedom and mobility that riding a motorcycle can give you. The following three things will help you achieve your goal – getting your licence.

- Acquire knowledge of the rules through your instructor and by carefully studying *The Highway Code*. A key element is to test and reinforce your knowledge. We're here to help you become a careful and safe motorcycle rider and we've designed this book to help you take the first step towards achieving your goal – preparing for your Theory Test.
- Take the right attitude. Be careful, courteous and considerate to all other road users.
- Learn and understand the skills of riding a motorcycle by taking lessons from a trained and fully qualified motorcycle instructor.

Six essential steps to getting your motorcycle licence

1. Get your provisional licence

If you haven't got a driving licence already, you will need a provisional licence to undertake motorcycle-riding instruction and ride on the road. You can apply for a provisional licence by post by using application forms D1 available from the Post Office. The provisional licence is issued in the form of a two-part document: a photo card and paper counterpart. To legally begin learning to ride, at the appropriate date, you must be in possession of the correct licence documents. Take care when completing all the forms. Many licences cannot be issued for the required date because of errors or omissions on the application forms. You will have to provide proof of identity such as a UK passport; make sure you have all the documents needed. You can also apply for your provisional licence online at **www.direct.gov.uk/motoring.** For more information about applying for a provisional licence contact the Driver Vehicle Licensing Agency (DVLA) on:

Tel 0870 240 0009
Minicom 01792 782 787
Fax 01792783 071
Online www.dvla.gov.uk; www.direct.gov.uk/motoring
By Post Drivers Customer Services (DCS) Correspondence Team, DVLA, Longview Road, Swansea SA6 7JL

2. Learn The Highway Code

The Highway Code is essential reading for all road users not just those learning to ride. It sets out all the rules for safe motorcycle riding, as well as the rules for other road users such as car drivers and pedestrians. When you have learned the rules you will be able to answer most of the questions in the Theory Test.

3. Take the Theory Test

The motorcycle test is in four parts: Compulsory Basic Training (CBT), the Theory Test (multiple-choice questions, case studies and hazard perception clips) and the Practical Tests (Module 1 Off Road and Module 2 On Road). Once you have a valid provisional or driving licence you may take your CBT and Theory Test at any time, but you must pass both tests before you are allowed to apply for Module 1 of the Practical Test. Once you have passed this test you can apply to take Module 2 of the Practical Test.

Useful Tip
The majority of training schools require that you pass the Theory Test prior to taking practical training.

You can book your Theory Test by post, telephone or online. To book your test you will need your provisional licence number and a credit or debit card. You will be given a test date immediately. To book your test by post you will need to fill in an application form, available from theory test centres or your motorcycle instructor or by calling the booking number below. Forms need to be sent to the address on the application form with a cheque, postal order, credit or debit card details. You should receive a test date within 10 days.

Tel 0300 200 1122; 0300 200 1133 (Welsh speakers)
Minicom 0300 200 1166
Fax 0300 200 1177
Online www.direct.gov.uk/drivingtest

Don't Forget
You'll need to take the following original documents with you to the Theory Test centre or you won't be allowed to take your Theory Test and will lose your exam fee.
Either your
- signed photo card licence and paper counterpart or
- signed provisional licence and passport

4. Compulsory Basic Training (CBT)

You cannot take your Practical Test until you have completed your Compulsory Basic Training (CBT). You can only use a training centre that has been approved by the Driving Standards Agency (DSA). Find approved CBT courses in your local area by contacting the DSA (**www.direct.gov.uk/motoring**), your local Road Safety Officer or motorcycle dealer.

CBT is a one-day training course that includes classroom and riding skills. The CBT, once successfully completed, provides the rider with a Certificate. This is valid for two years and in conjunction with the provisional motorcycle licence entitles the rider to ride up to a 125cc machine (50cc for 16 year olds) with 'L' plates. The rider, however, cannot carry a pillion passenger or use motorways.

5. Take the Practical Test

Once you have passed CBT and the Theory Test, and with your instructor's guidance based on your progress, you can plan ahead for a suitable test date for Module 1 and then Module 2 of the Practical Test.

The majority of motorcycle riders learn the necessary riding skills quite quickly and most training courses are between 3 to 5 days, depending on the rider's ability. Ensure the full official syllabus is covered and, as your skills develop, get as much practice as possible. (See page 8 or visit **www.direct.gov.uk/motoring** for minimum test vehicle requirements to make sure that you take your Practical Test (Modules 1 and 2) on the size of motorcycle that you intend to ride.)

You can book your Practical Test online or by phone at any time between 8am and 6pm Monday to Friday. You can pay for your test using a credit or debit card (the person who books the test must be the cardholder). If you need to, you can change your Practical Test appointment by phone or online.

Tel 0300 200 1122; 0300 200 1133 (Welsh speakers)
Minicom 0300 200 1144
Fax 0300 200 1155
Online www.direct.gov.uk/drivingtest

Make sure you have the following details to hand when booking your Practical Test.
• Theory Test pass certificate number
• driver number shown on your licence
• your preferred date
• unacceptable days or periods
• if you can accept a test at short notice
• disability or any special circumstances
• your credit/debit card details

6. Apply for your full driver's licence

After you have passed your Practical Test your examiner will send your provisional or driving licence and test certificate to the DVLA and you will receive your licence by post within four weeks of passing Module 2 of your Practical Test. When you receive your licence, it is important that you check that the correct motorcycle category has been added on the reverse of your photo card licence.

Once you have taken and passed your Practical Test, you will receive one of four types of licence, depending on your age and the size of motorcycle that you used for your Practical Test (Modules 1 and 2).

Category P (minimum age 16) This category is for mopeds with an engine size of up to 50cc and a maximum speed of up to 50km per hour.

Category A1 (age 17 and over) If you pass the Practical Test on a category A1 'light motorcycle' (75–125cc), you can ride a motorcycle up to 125cc with a maximum output of 14.6bhp without 'L' plates.

Category A – Standard Motorcycle If you are under the age of 21, then the largest size motorcycle you can take your test on is a 125cc. If you pass the Practical Test on a category A 'standard motorcycle' (121–125cc), you can ride any motorcycle but the power output must be restricted to a maximum output of 33.3bhp. After two years the restriction is automatically lifted and you can ride any motorcycle with any power output.

Category A – Larger Motorcycle If you are over 21, you can train and take your Practical Test on a larger motorcycle, usually 500–650cc (power output minimum of 46.6bhp), and have a full licence for any motorcycle.

The Theory Test: What to expect

How to use this book

This book will help you to prepare for the multiple-choice questions and case studies parts of the Theory Test and tell you what to expect in the hazard perception clips part.

In this book you will find:
- The questions and answers are arranged under the 14 official DSA syllabus topics.
- Questions dealing with related aspects of a topic are grouped together and shown by a colour-coded band.
- Each question includes a tick box so you can test your skills.
- All the correct answers are at the back of the book.

Questions marked with an **NI** symbol are those **not** found in the Theory Test in Northern Ireland

This book contains all the official questions for motorcycle riders, which appear in the official Theory Test question bank of the DSA. You could be tested on any of these questions, from a range of topics and in any order when you take your touch-screen Theory Test.

The questions are arranged in topics, such as Safety Margins and Rules of the Road. Each topic has its own colour band to help you find your way around. However, as you start to work through the questions you will soon discover that similar questions on a similar subject may appear in different sections. Don't be put off by this, but read each question and the choice of answers very carefully. Similar questions may be asked in a slightly different way to test your knowledge.

Experience has taught us that learners find particular questions difficult and are often confused when they see questions, which are similar. However, most of the questions can be answered if you learn *The Highway Code*. Although, you will only find the answers to some questions by talking to your instructor and learning about good riding practice on the road.

You'll find all the correct answers to the questions at the back of the book, that way, you can easily test yourself to see what you are getting right and what you will need to work on.

Remember
- Don't try too many questions at once.
- Don't try to learn the answers by heart.
- The order of the questions in this book may be different from how they are arranged in the actual test – so don't try to memorise the order.

You'll also find a short glossary at the back of this book (pages 149–155), which explains some of the more difficult words and terms used in the theory questions and *The Highway Code*. It is in alphabetical order and you can use this to check if you're not sure what a chicane is, for example, or what tailgating means.

What to expect in the multiple-choice test

You will have 57 minutes to complete the questions in the test, using a touch-screen to select your answers. The test is a set of 50 questions drawn from a bank of more than 800, all of which have multiple-choice answers. In order to pass the test you must answer a minimum of 43 questions correctly within the given time. The Government may change the pass mark from time to time. The DSA will be able to tell you if there has been a change.

How to answer the questions

The questions appear on the screen one at a time and you can return to any of the questions within the 57 minutes to re-check or alter your answers. Each question has four, five or six possible answers. You must mark the boxes with the correct answer(s). Each question tells you how many answers to mark. Don't worry about accidentally missing marking an answer because you will be reminded that you haven't ticked enough boxes before moving on to the next question. Some of the questions will take the form of a case study (see page 12).

Study each question carefully, making sure you understand what it is asking you. Look carefully at any diagram, drawing or photograph. Before you look at the answers given, decide what you think the correct answer(s) might be. You can then select the answer(s) that matches the one you had decided on. If you follow this system, you will avoid being confused by answers that appear to be similar.

You can also answer the questions in any order you choose by moving forwards and backwards through the questions. You can also change your answer(s) if necessary and flag questions you're unsure about, then go back to them later in the test. Your remaining time is shown on the screen throughout the test.

Useful Tip

You have the option to have a 15-minute practice session using the computer before your real test starts. If you have enough time at the end of the test, you will be able to use the review button to check all your answers before finishing the test.

Case study questions

A case study was introduced to the multiple-choice part of the Theory Test in September 2009, and are designed to test that you have not only learned your motorcycle riding theory but that you understand how to apply the theory in a given riding situation.

Typically, five of the 50 questions in the Theory Test will take the form of a case study. All five questions will be based on a single road scenario and appear one at time. The case study questions are taken from the DSA's databank of Theory Test Questions (see pages 17–148) and have multiple-choice answers.

The case study in your Theory Test exam could be based on any riding situation and you could be asked questions from a range of topics covered by the Theory Test syllabus. The following example has been put together by the AA to demonstrate how the case study will work in the 'real exam', so you'll know what to expect. This example will not appear in the Theory Test.

CASE STUDY 1

You need to visit a relative in a hospital some distance from where you live. The journey will take you on various roads including both A-roads and motorways.

As you start your journey it begins to rain and continues to get heavier as you ride.

You have not ridden to the hospital before but you have planned your route before leaving and feel confident about the journey.

1. You are following a vehicle on a wet road. You should leave a time gap of at least

Mark one answer

☐ one second

☐ two seconds

☐ three seconds

☐ four seconds

Back   Flag   Review   Next

CASE STUDY 1

You need to visit a relative in a hospital some distance from where you live. The journey will take you on various roads including both A-roads and motorways.

As you start your journey it begins to rain and continues to get heavier as you ride.

You have not ridden to the hospital before but you have planned your route before leaving and feel confident about the journey.

2. What does this sign mean?

Mark one answer

☐ you have priority

☐ no motor vehicles

☐ two-way traffic

☐ no overtaking

Back

CASE STUDY 1

You need to visit a relative in a hospital some distance from where you live. The journey will take you on various roads including both A-roads and motorways.

As you start your journey it begins to rain and continues to get heavier as you ride.

You have not ridden to the hospital before but you have planned your route before leaving and feel confident about the journey.

3. You have just gone through deep water. To dry off the brakes you should

Mark one answer

☐ accelerate and keep to a high speed for a short time

☐ go slowly while gently applying the brakes

☐ avoid using the brakes at all for a few miles

☐ stop for at least an hour to allow them time to dry

Back   Flag   Review   Next

CASE STUDY 1

You need to visit a relative in a hospital some distance from where you live. The journey will take you on various roads including both A-roads and motorways.

As you start your journey it begins to rain and continues to get heavier as you ride.

You have not ridden to the hospital before but you have planned your route before leaving and feel confident about the journey.

4. A bus has stopped at a bus stop ahead of you. Its right-hand indicator is flashing. You should

Mark one answer

☐ flash your headlights and slow down

☐ slow down and give way if it is safe to do so

☐ sound your horn and keep going

☐ slow down and then sound your horn

Next

CASE STUDY 1

You need to visit a relative in a hospital some distance from where you live. The journey will take you on various roads including both A-roads and motorways.

As you start your journey it begins to rain and continues to get heavier as you ride.

You have not ridden to the hospital before but you have planned your route before leaving and feel confident about the journey.

5. Where you see street lights but no speed limit signs the limit is usually

Mark one answer

☐ 30mph

☐ 40mph

☐ 50mph

☐ 60mph

Back   Flag   Review   Next

Answers to sample case study questions: 1D 2D 3B 4B 5A

What to expect in the hazard perception test

After a break of up to three minutes you will begin the hazard perception part of the test. This test lasts for about 20 minutes. Before you start you will be given some instructions explaining how the test works; you'll also get a chance to practise with the computer and mouse before you start the test.

Next you will see 14 film or video clips of real street scenes with traffic such as cars, pedestrians, cyclists, etc. The scenes are shot from the point of view of a rider on a motorcycle. You have to notice potential hazards that are developing on the road ahead – that is, problems that could lead to an accident. As soon as you notice a hazard developing, click the mouse. You will have plenty of time to see the hazard – but the sooner you notice it, the more marks you score. Each clip has at least one hazard in it – some clips may have more than one hazard. You have to score a minimum of 44 out of 75 to pass, but the pass mark may change so check with your instructor or the DSA before sitting your test.

Be Aware
- The computer has checks built in to show anyone trying to cheat – for example someone who keeps clicking the mouse all the time.
- Unlike the multiple-choice questions, you will not have an opportunity to go back to an earlier clip and change your response, so you need to concentrate throughout the test.

Although you won't be able to practise using the actual clips used in the hazard perception test, of course, a range of training books, practice DVDs and CD ROMs are widely available to help you prepare for this part of the Theory Test.

Above: Real road scenes feature in the video clips in the hazard perception test
Right: Click the mouse when you spot potential hazards – the pedestrian crossing the side road and the cyclist approaching a parked vehicle (ringed in yellow). Click again as the hazard develops when the cyclist (ringed in red) moves out to overtake the parked vehicle.

Theory Test Questions

1 You want to change lanes in busy, moving traffic. Why could looking over your shoulder help?

Mark two answers

- [ ] **A.** Mirrors may not cover blind spots
- [ ] **B.** To avoid having to give a signal
- [ ] **C.** So traffic ahead will make room for you
- [ ] **D.** So your balance will not be affected
- [ ] **E.** Drivers behind you would be warned

2 You are about to turn right. What should you do just before you turn?

Mark one answer

- [ ] **A.** Give the correct signal
- [ ] **B.** Take a 'lifesaver' glance over your shoulder
- [ ] **C.** Select the correct gear
- [ ] **D.** Get in position ready for the turn

3 What is the 'lifesaver' when riding a motorcycle?

Mark one answer

- [ ] **A.** A certificate every motorcyclist must have
- [ ] **B.** A final rearward glance before changing direction
- [ ] **C.** A part of the motorcycle tool kit
- [ ] **D.** A mirror fitted to check blind spots

4 You see road signs showing a sharp bend ahead. What should you do?

Mark one answer

- [ ] **A.** Continue at the same speed
- [ ] **B.** Slow down as you go around the bend
- [ ] **C.** Slow down as you come out of the bend
- [ ] **D.** Slow down before the bend

5 You are riding at night and are dazzled by the headlights of an oncoming car. You should

Mark one answer

- [ ] **A.** slow down or stop
- [ ] **B.** close your eyes
- [ ] **C.** flash your headlight
- [ ] **D.** turn your head away

6 When riding, your shoulders obstruct the view in your mirrors. To overcome this you should

Mark one answer

- [ ] **A.** indicate earlier than normal
- [ ] **B.** fit smaller mirrors
- [ ] **C.** extend the mirror arms
- [ ] **D.** brake earlier than normal

7 On a motorcycle you should only use a mobile telephone when you

Mark one answer

- [ ] **A.** have a pillion passenger to help
- [ ] **B.** have parked in a safe place
- [ ] **C.** have a motorcycle with automatic gears
- [ ] **D.** are travelling on a quiet road

8 You are riding at night. You have your headlight on main beam. Another vehicle is overtaking you. When should you dip your headlight?

Mark one answer

- [ ] **A.** When the other vehicle signals to overtake
- [ ] **B.** As soon as the other vehicle moves out to overtake
- [ ] **C.** As soon as the other vehicle passes you
- [ ] **D.** After the other vehicle pulls in front of you

9 To move off safely from a parked position you should

Mark one answer

- A. signal if other drivers will need to slow down
- B. leave your motorcycle on its stand until the road is clear
- C. give an arm signal as well as using your indicators
- D. look over your shoulder for a final check

10 In motorcycling, the term 'lifesaver' refers to

Mark one answer

- A. a final rearward glance
- B. an approved safety helmet
- C. a reflective jacket
- D. the two-second rule

11 Riding a motorcycle when you are cold could cause you to

Mark one answer

- A. be more alert
- B. be more relaxed
- C. react more quickly
- D. lose concentration

12 You are riding at night and are dazzled by the lights of an approaching vehicle. What should you do?

Mark one answer

- A. Switch off your headlight
- B. Switch to main beam
- C. Slow down and stop
- D. Flash your headlight

13 You should always check the 'blind areas' before

Mark one answer

- A. moving off
- B. slowing down
- C. changing gear
- D. giving a signal

14 The 'blind area' should be checked before

Mark one answer

- A. giving a signal
- B. applying the brakes
- C. changing direction
- D. giving an arm signal

15 It is vital to check the 'blind area' before

Mark one answer

- A. changing gear
- B. giving signals
- C. slowing down
- D. changing lanes

16 You are about to emerge from a junction. Your pillion passenger tells you it's clear. When should you rely on their judgement?

Mark one answer

- A. Never, you should always look for yourself
- B. When the roads are very busy
- C. When the roads are very quiet
- D. Only when they are a qualified rider

17 You are about to emerge from a junction. Your pillion passenger tells you it's safe to go. What should you do?

Mark one answer

- A. Go if you are sure they can see clearly
- B. Check for yourself before pulling out
- C. Take their advice and ride on
- D. Ask them to check again before you go

18 What must you do before stopping normally?

Mark one answer

- A. Put both feet down
- B. Select first gear
- C. Use your mirrors
- D. Move into neutral

19 You have been waiting for some time to make a right turn into a side road. What should you do just before you make the turn?

Mark one answer

- A. Move close to the kerb
- B. Select a higher gear
- C. Make a 'lifesaver' check
- D. Wave to the oncoming traffic

20 You are turning right onto a dual carriageway. What should you do before emerging?

Mark one answer

- A. Stop, and then select a very low gear
- B. Position in the left gutter of the side road
- C. Check that the central reservation is wide enough
- D. Check there is enough room for vehicles behind you

21 When riding a different motorcycle you should

Mark one answer

- A. ask someone to ride with you for the first time
- B. ride as soon as possible, as all controls and switches are the same
- C. leave your gloves behind so switches can be operated more easily
- D. be sure you know where all controls and switches are

22 Why can it be helpful to have mirrors fitted on each side of your motorcycle?

Mark one answer

- A. To judge the gap when filtering in traffic
- B. To give protection when riding in poor weather
- C. To make your motorcycle appear larger to other drivers
- D. To give you the best view of the road behind

23 Before you make a U-turn in the road, you should

Mark one answer

- A. give an arm signal as well as using your indicators
- B. signal so that other drivers can slow down for you
- C. look over your shoulder for a final check
- D. select a higher gear than normal

24 As you approach this bridge you should

Mark three answers

- A. move into the middle of the road to get a better view
- B. slow down
- C. get over the bridge as quickly as possible
- D. consider using your horn
- E. find another route
- F. beware of pedestrians

25 When following a large vehicle you should keep well back because this

Mark one answer

- A. allows you to corner more quickly
- B. helps the large vehicle to stop more easily
- C. allows the driver to see you in the mirrors
- D. helps you to keep out of the wind

26 In which of these situations should you avoid overtaking?

Mark one answer

- A. Just after a bend
- B. In a one-way street
- C. On a 30mph road
- D. Approaching a dip in the road

27 This road marking warns

Mark one answer

- A. drivers to use the hard shoulder
- B. overtaking drivers there is a bend to the left
- C. overtaking drivers to move back to the left
- D. drivers that it is safe to overtake

28 Your mobile phone rings while you are travelling. You should

Mark one answer

- A. stop immediately
- B. answer it immediately
- C. pull up in a suitable place
- D. pull up at the nearest kerb

29 Why are these yellow lines painted across the road?

Mark one answer

- A. To help you choose the correct lane
- B. To help you keep the correct separation distance
- C. To make you aware of your speed
- D. To tell you the distance to the roundabout

30 You are approaching traffic lights that have been on green for some time. You should

Mark one answer

- A. accelerate hard
- B. maintain your speed
- C. be ready to stop
- D. brake hard

31 Which of the following should you do before stopping?

Mark one answer

- A. Sound the horn
- B. Use the mirrors
- C. Select a higher gear
- D. Flash your headlights

32 When you see a hazard ahead you should use the mirrors. Why is this?

Mark one answer

- [ ] **A.** Because you will need to accelerate out of danger
- [ ] **B.** To assess how your actions will affect following traffic
- [ ] **C.** Because you will need to brake sharply to a stop
- [ ] **D.** To check what is happening on the road ahead

33 You are waiting to turn right at the end of a road. Your view is obstructed by parked vehicles. What should you do?

Mark one answer

- [ ] **A.** Stop and then move forward slowly and carefully for a proper view
- [ ] **B.** Move quickly to where you can see so you only block traffic from one direction
- [ ] **C.** Wait for a pedestrian to let you know when it is safe for you to emerge
- [ ] **D.** Turn your vehicle around immediately and find another junction to use

34 You are turning right at a large roundabout. Before you leave the roundabout you should

Mark one answer

- [ ] **A.** take a 'lifesaver' glance over your left shoulder
- [ ] **B.** give way to all traffic from the right
- [ ] **C.** put on your right indicator
- [ ] **D.** cancel the left indicator

35 You are turning right at a large roundabout. Before you cross a lane to reach your exit you should

Mark one answer

- [ ] **A.** take a 'lifesaver' glance over your right shoulder
- [ ] **B.** put on your right indicator
- [ ] **C.** take a 'lifesaver' glance over your left shoulder
- [ ] **D.** cancel the left indicator

36 You are positioned to turn right on a multi-lane roundabout. What should you do before moving to a lane on your left?

Mark one answer

- [ ] **A.** Take a 'lifesaver' glance over your right shoulder
- [ ] **B.** Cancel the left signal
- [ ] **C.** Signal to the right
- [ ] **D.** Take a 'lifesaver' glance over your left shoulder

37 You are turning right on a multi-lane roundabout. When should you take a 'lifesaver' glance over your left shoulder?

Mark one answer

- [ ] **A.** After moving into the left lane
- [ ] **B.** After leaving the roundabout
- [ ] **C.** Before signalling to the right
- [ ] **D.** Before moving into the left lane

38 You are on a motorway. You see an incident on the other side of the road. Your lane is clear. You should

Mark one answer

- [ ] **A.** assist the emergency services
- [ ] **B.** stop, and cross the road to help
- [ ] **C.** concentrate on what is happening ahead
- [ ] **D.** place a warning triangle in the road

39 You are riding towards a zebra crossing. Pedestrians are waiting to cross. You should

Mark one answer

- [ ] **A.** give way to the elderly and infirm only
- [ ] **B.** slow down and prepare to stop
- [ ] **C.** use your headlight to indicate they can cross
- [ ] **D.** wave at them to cross the road

40 You are riding a motorcycle and following a large vehicle at 40mph. You should position yourself

Mark one answer

- [ ] **A.** close behind to make it easier to overtake the vehicle
- [ ] **B.** to the left of the road to make it easier to be seen
- [ ] **C.** close behind the vehicle to keep out of the wind
- [ ] **D.** well back so that you can see past the vehicle

41 You are riding on a country road. Two horses with riders are in the distance. You should

Mark one answer

- [ ] **A.** continue at your normal speed
- [ ] **B.** change down the gears quickly
- [ ] **C.** slow down and be ready to stop
- [ ] **D.** flash your headlight to warn them

42 You are approaching a red light at a puffin crossing. Pedestrians are on the crossing. The red light will stay on until

Mark one answer

- [ ] **A.** you start to edge forward on to the crossing
- [ ] **B.** the pedestrians have reached a safe position
- [ ] **C.** the pedestrians are clear of the front of your motorcycle
- [ ] **D.** a driver from the opposite direction reaches the crossing

43 You are riding a slow-moving scooter on a narrow winding road. You should

Mark one answer

- [ ] **A.** keep well out to stop vehicles overtaking dangerously
- [ ] **B.** wave vehicles behind you to pass, if you think they can overtake quickly
- [ ] **C.** pull in safely when you can, to let vehicles behind you overtake
- [ ] **D.** give a left signal when it is safe for vehicles to overtake you

44 When riding a motorcycle your normal road position should allow

Mark two answers

- [ ] **A.** other vehicles to overtake on your left
- [ ] **B.** the driver ahead to see you in their mirrors
- [ ] **C.** you to prevent vehicles behind from overtaking
- [ ] **D.** you to be seen by traffic that is emerging from junctions ahead
- [ ] **E.** you to ride within half a metre (1 foot 8 inches) of the kerb

45 At a pelican crossing the flashing amber light means you MUST

Mark one answer

- A. stop and wait for the green light
- B. stop and wait for the red light
- C. give way to pedestrians waiting to cross
- D. give way to pedestrians already on the crossing

46 You should never wave people across at pedestrian crossings because

Mark one answer

- A. there may be another vehicle coming
- B. they may not be looking
- C. it is safer for you to carry on
- D. they may not be ready to cross

47 At a puffin crossing, which colour follows the green signal?

Mark one answer

- A. Steady red
- B. Flashing amber
- C. Steady amber
- D. Flashing green

48 The conditions are good and dry. You could use the 'two-second rule'

Mark one answer

- A. before restarting the engine after it has stalled
- B. to keep a safe gap from the vehicle in front
- C. before using the 'Mirror-Signal-Manoeuvre' routine
- D. when emerging on wet roads

49 'Tailgating' means

Mark one answer

- A. using the rear door of a hatchback car
- B. reversing into a parking space
- C. following another vehicle too closely
- D. driving with rear fog lights on

50 Following this vehicle too closely is unwise because

Mark one answer

- A. your brakes will overheat
- B. your view ahead is increased
- C. your engine will overheat
- D. your view ahead is reduced

51 You are following a vehicle on a wet road. You should leave a time gap of at least

Mark one answer

- A. one second
- B. two seconds
- C. three seconds
- D. four seconds

52 You are in a line of traffic. The driver behind you is following very closely. What action should you take?

Mark one answer

- A. Ignore the following driver and continue to travel within the speed limit
- B. Slow down, gradually increasing the gap between you and the vehicle in front
- C. Signal left and wave the following driver past
- D. Move over to a position just left of the centre line of the road

53 A long, heavily laden lorry is taking a long time to overtake you. What should you do?

Mark one answer

- A. Speed up
- B. Slow down
- C. Hold your speed
- D. Change direction

54 Which of the following vehicles will use blue flashing beacons?

Mark three answers

- A. Motorway maintenance
- B. Bomb disposal
- C. Blood transfusion
- D. Police patrol
- E. Breakdown recovery

55 Which THREE of these emergency services might have blue flashing beacons?

Mark three answers

- A. Coastguard
- B. Bomb disposal
- C. Gritting lorries
- D. Animal ambulances
- E. Mountain rescue
- F. Doctors' cars

56 When being followed by an ambulance showing a flashing blue beacon you should

Mark one answer

- A. pull over as soon as safely possible to let it pass
- B. accelerate hard to get away from it
- C. maintain your speed and course
- D. brake harshly and immediately stop in the road

57 What type of emergency vehicle is fitted with a green flashing beacon?

Mark one answer

- A. Fire engine
- B. Road gritter
- C. Ambulance
- D. Doctor's car

58 A flashing green beacon on a vehicle means

Mark one answer

- A. police on non-urgent duties
- B. doctor on an emergency call
- C. road safety patrol operating
- D. gritting in progress

59 A vehicle has a flashing green beacon. What does this mean?

Mark one answer

- A. A doctor is answering an emergency call
- B. The vehicle is slow moving
- C. It is a motorway police patrol vehicle
- D. The vehicle is carrying hazardous chemicals

60 Diamond-shaped signs give instructions to

Mark one answer

- A. tram drivers
- B. bus drivers
- C. lorry drivers
- D. taxi drivers

30

61 On a road where trams operate, which of these vehicles will be most at risk from the tram rails?

Mark one answer

- **A.** Cars
- **B.** Cycles
- **C.** Buses
- **D.** Lorries

62 What should you use your horn for?

Mark one answer

- **A.** To alert others to your presence
- **B.** To allow you right of way
- **C.** To greet other road users
- **D.** To signal your annoyance

63 You are in a one-way street and want to turn right. You should position yourself

Mark one answer

- **A.** in the right-hand lane
- **B.** in the left-hand lane
- **C.** in either lane, depending on the traffic
- **D.** just left of the centre line

64 You wish to turn right ahead. Why should you take up the correct position in good time?

Mark one answer

- **A.** To allow other drivers to pull out in front of you
- **B.** To give a better view into the road that you're joining
- **C.** To help other road users know what you intend to do
- **D.** To allow drivers to pass you on the right

65 At which type of crossing are cyclists allowed to ride across with pedestrians?

Mark one answer

- **A.** Toucan
- **B.** Puffin
- **C.** Pelican
- **D.** Zebra

66 A bus has stopped at a bus stop ahead of you. Its right-hand indicator is flashing. You should

Mark one answer

- **A.** flash your headlights and slow down
- **B.** slow down and give way if it is safe to do so
- **C.** sound your horn and keep going
- **D.** slow down and then sound your horn

67 You are travelling at the legal speed limit. A vehicle comes up quickly behind, flashing its headlights. You should

Mark one answer

- **A.** accelerate to make a gap behind you
- **B.** touch the brakes sharply to show your brake lights
- **C.** maintain your speed to prevent the vehicle from overtaking
- **D.** allow the vehicle to overtake

68 You should ONLY flash your headlights to other road users

Mark one answer

- [ ] **A.** to show that you are giving way
- [ ] **B.** to show that you are about to turn
- [ ] **C.** to tell them that you have right of way
- [ ] **D.** to let them know that you are there

69 You are approaching unmarked crossroads. How should you deal with this type of junction?

Mark one answer

- [ ] **A.** Accelerate and keep to the middle
- [ ] **B.** Slow down and keep to the right
- [ ] **C.** Accelerate looking to the left
- [ ] **D.** Slow down and look both ways

70 You are approaching a pelican crossing. The amber light is flashing. You must

Mark one answer

- [ ] **A.** give way to pedestrians who are crossing
- [ ] **B.** encourage pedestrians to cross
- [ ] **C.** not move until the green light appears
- [ ] **D.** stop even if the crossing is clear

71 Young, inexperienced and newly qualified motorcyclists can often be involved in crashes. This is due to

Mark one answer

- [ ] **A.** being too cautious at junctions
- [ ] **B.** riding in the middle of their lane
- [ ] **C.** showing off and being competitive
- [ ] **D.** wearing full weather protection

72 A loose drive chain on a motorcycle could cause

Mark one answer
- [ ] **A.** the front wheel to wobble
- [ ] **B.** the ignition to cut out
- [ ] **C.** the brakes to fail
- [ ] **D.** the rear wheel to lock

73 What is the most important reason why you should keep your motorcycle regularly maintained?

Mark one answer
- [ ] **A.** To accelerate faster than other traffic
- [ ] **B.** So the motorcycle can carry panniers
- [ ] **C.** To keep the machine roadworthy
- [ ] **D.** So the motorcycle can carry a passenger

74 How should you ride a motorcycle when NEW tyres have just been fitted?

Mark one answer
- [ ] **A.** Carefully, until the shiny surface is worn off
- [ ] **B.** By braking hard especially into bends
- [ ] **C.** Through normal riding with higher air pressures
- [ ] **D.** By riding at faster than normal speeds

75 Which of the following would NOT make you more visible in daylight?

Mark one answer
- [ ] **A.** Wearing a black helmet
- [ ] **B.** Wearing a white helmet
- [ ] **C.** Switching on your dipped headlight
- [ ] **D.** Wearing a fluorescent jacket

76 When riding and wearing brightly coloured clothing you will

Mark one answer
- [ ] **A.** dazzle other motorists on the road
- [ ] **B.** be seen more easily by other motorists
- [ ] **C.** create a hazard by distracting other drivers
- [ ] **D.** be able to ride on unlit roads at night with sidelights

77 You are riding a motorcycle in very hot weather. You should

Mark one answer
- [ ] **A.** ride with your visor fully open
- [ ] **B.** continue to wear protective clothing
- [ ] **C.** wear trainers instead of boots
- [ ] **D.** slacken your helmet strap

78 Why should you wear fluorescent clothing when riding in daylight?

Mark one answer
- [ ] **A.** It reduces wind resistance
- [ ] **B.** It prevents injury if you come off the machine
- [ ] **C.** It helps other road users to see you
- [ ] **D.** It keeps you cool in hot weather

79 Why should riders wear reflective clothing?

Mark one answer

A. To protect them from the cold
B. To protect them from direct sunlight
C. To be seen better in daylight
D. To be seen better at night

80 Which of the following fairings would give you the best weather protection?

Mark one answer

A. Handlebar
B. Sports
C. Touring
D. Windscreen

81 It would be illegal to ride with a helmet on when

Mark one answer

A. the helmet is not fastened correctly
B. the helmet is more than four years old
C. you have borrowed someone else's helmet
D. the helmet does not have chin protection

82 Your visor becomes badly scratched. You should

Mark one answer

A. polish it with a fine abrasive
B. replace it
C. wash it in soapy water
D. clean it with petrol

83 The legal minimum depth of tread for motorcycle tyres is

Mark one answer

A. 1mm
B. 1.6mm
C. 2.5mm
D. 4mm

84 Which of the following makes it easier for motorcyclists to be seen?

Mark three answers

A. Using a dipped headlight
B. Wearing a fluorescent jacket
C. Wearing a white helmet
D. Wearing a grey helmet
E. Wearing black leathers
F. Using a tinted visor

85 Tyre pressures should be increased on your motorcycle when

Mark one answer

A. riding on a wet road
B. carrying a pillion passenger
C. travelling on an uneven surface
D. riding on twisty roads

86 Your oil light comes on as you are riding. You should

Mark one answer

A. go to a dealer for an oil change
B. go to the nearest garage for their advice
C. ride slowly for a few miles to see if the light goes out
D. stop as quickly as possible and try to find the cause

87 When may you have to increase the tyre pressures on your motorcycle?

Mark three answers

- A. When carrying a passenger
- B. After a long journey
- C. When carrying a load
- D. When riding at high speeds
- E. When riding in hot weather

88 Which TWO of these items on a motorcycle MUST be kept clean?

Mark two answers

- A. Number plate
- B. Wheels
- C. Engine
- D. Fairing
- E. Headlight

89 Motorcycle tyres MUST

Mark two answers

- A. have the same tread pattern
- B. be correctly inflated
- C. be the same size, front and rear
- D. both be the same make
- E. have sufficient tread depth

90 You should use the engine cut-out switch on your motorcycle to

Mark one answer

- A. save wear and tear on the battery
- B. stop the engine for a short time
- C. stop the engine in an emergency
- D. save wear and tear on the ignition

91 Riding your motorcycle with a slack or worn drive chain may cause

Mark one answer

- A. an engine misfire
- B. early tyre wear
- C. increased emissions
- D. a locked wheel

92 You have adjusted the tension on your drive chain. You should check the

Mark one answer

- A. rear wheel alignment
- B. tyre pressures
- C. valve clearances
- D. sidelights

93 You forget to switch the choke off after the engine warms up. This could

Mark one answer

- A. flatten the battery
- B. reduce braking distances
- C. use less fuel
- D. cause much more engine wear

94 When riding your motorcycle a tyre bursts. What should you do?

Mark one answer
- A. Slow gently to a stop
- B. Brake firmly to a stop
- C. Change to a high gear
- D. Lower the side stand

95 A motorcycle engine that is properly maintained will

Mark one answer
- A. use much more fuel
- B. have lower exhaust emissions
- C. increase your insurance premiums
- D. not need to have an MOT

96 What should you clean visors and goggles with?

Mark one answer
- A. Petrol
- B. White spirit
- C. Antifreeze
- D. Soapy water

97 You are riding on a quiet road. Your visor fogs up. What should you do?

Mark one answer
- A. Continue at a reduced speed
- B. Stop as soon as possible and wipe it
- C. Build up speed to increase air flow
- D. Close the helmet air vents

98 You are riding in hot weather. What is the safest type of footwear?

Mark one answer
- A. Sandals
- B. Trainers
- C. Shoes
- D. Boots

99 A friend offers you a second-hand safety helmet for you to use. Why may this be a bad idea?

Mark one answer
- A. It may be damaged
- B. You will be breaking the law
- C. You will affect your insurance cover
- D. It may be a full-face type

100 Which of the following should not be used to fasten your safety helmet?

Mark one answer

- A. Double D ring fastening
- B. Velcro tab
- C. Quick release fastening
- D. Bar and buckle

101 After warming up the engine you leave the choke ON. What will this do?

Mark one answer

- A. Discharge the battery
- B. Use more fuel
- C. Improve handling
- D. Use less fuel

102 You want to ride your motorcycle in the dark. What could you wear to be seen more easily?

Mark two answers

- A. A black leather jacket
- B. Reflective clothing
- C. A white helmet
- D. A red helmet

103 You are riding a motorcycle of more than 50cc. Which FOUR would make a tyre illegal?

Mark four answers

- A. Tread less than 1.6mm deep
- B. Tread less than 1mm deep
- C. A large bulge in the wall
- D. A recut tread
- E. Exposed ply or cord
- F. A stone wedged in the tread

104 You should maintain cable-operated brakes

Mark two answers

- A. by regular adjustment when necessary
- B. at normal service times only
- C. yearly, before taking the motorcycle for its MOT
- D. by oiling cables and pivots regularly

105 A properly serviced motorcycle will give

Mark two answers

- A. lower insurance premiums
- B. a refund on your road tax
- C. better fuel economy
- D. cleaner exhaust emissions

106 Your motorcycle has a catalytic converter. Its purpose is to reduce

Mark one answer

- A. exhaust noise
- B. fuel consumption
- C. exhaust emissions
- D. engine noise

107 Refitting which of the following will disturb your wheel alignment?

Mark one answer

- A. front wheel
- B. front brakes
- C. rear brakes
- D. rear wheel

108 After refitting your rear wheel what should you check?

Mark one answer

- A. Your steering damper
- B. Your side stand
- C. Your wheel alignment
- D. Your suspension preload

109 You are checking your direction indicators. How often per second must they flash?

Mark one answer

- A. Between 1 and 2 times
- B. Between 3 and 4 times
- C. Between 5 and 6 times
- D. Between 7 and 8 times

110 After adjusting the final drive chain what should you check?

Mark one answer

- A. The rear wheel alignment
- B. The suspension adjustment
- C. The rear shock absorber
- D. The front suspension forks

111 Your steering feels wobbly. Which of these is a likely cause?

Mark one answer

- A. Tyre pressure is too high
- B. Incorrectly adjusted brakes
- C. Worn steering head bearings
- D. A broken clutch cable

112 You see oil on your front forks. Should you be concerned about this?

Mark one answer

- A. No, unless the amount of oil increases
- B. No, lubrication here is perfectly normal
- C. Yes, it is illegal to ride with an oil leak
- D. Yes, oil could drip on to your tyre

113 You have a faulty oil seal on a shock absorber. Why is this a serious problem?

Mark one answer

- A. It will cause excessive chain wear
- B. Dripping oil could reduce the grip of your tyre
- C. Your motorcycle will be harder to ride uphill
- D. Your motorcycle will not accelerate so quickly

114 Oil is leaking from your forks. Why should you NOT ride a motorcycle in this condition?

Mark one answer

- A. Your brakes could be affected by dripping oil
- B. Your steering is likely to seize up
- C. The forks will quickly begin to rust
- D. The motorcycle will become too noisy

115 You have adjusted your drive chain. If this is not done properly, what problem could it cause?

Mark one answer
- [ ] **A.** Inaccurate speedometer reading
- [ ] **B.** Loss of braking power
- [ ] **C.** Incorrect rear wheel alignment
- [ ] **D.** Excessive fuel consumption

116 You have adjusted your drive chain. Why is it also important to check rear wheel alignment?

Mark one answer
- [ ] **A.** Your tyre may be more likely to puncture
- [ ] **B.** Fuel consumption could be greatly increased
- [ ] **C.** You may not be able to reach top speed
- [ ] **D.** Your motorcycle could be unstable on bends

117 There is a cut in the sidewall of one of your tyres. What should you do about this?

Mark one answer
- [ ] **A.** Replace the tyre before riding the motorcycle
- [ ] **B.** Check regularly to see if it gets any worse
- [ ] **C.** Repair the puncture before riding the motorcycle
- [ ] **D.** Reduce pressure in the tyre before you ride

118 You need to put air into your tyres. How would you find out the correct pressure to use?

Mark one answer
- [ ] **A.** It will be shown on the tyre wall
- [ ] **B.** It will be stamped on the wheel
- [ ] **C.** By checking the vehicle owner's manual
- [ ] **D.** By checking the registration document

119 You can prevent a cable operated clutch from becoming stiff by keeping the cable

Mark one answer
- [ ] **A.** tight
- [ ] **B.** dry
- [ ] **C.** slack
- [ ] **D.** oiled

120 When adusting your chain it is important for the wheels to be aligned accurately. Incorrect wheel alignment can cause

Mark one answer
- [ ] **A.** a serious loss of power
- [ ] **B.** reduced braking performance
- [ ] **C.** increased tyre wear
- [ ] **D.** reduced ground clearance

121 What problem can incorrectly aligned wheels cause?

Mark one answer
- [ ] **A.** Faulty headlight adjustment
- [ ] **B.** Reduced braking performance
- [ ] **C.** Better ground clearance
- [ ] **D.** Instability when cornering

122 What is most likely to be affected by incorrect wheel alignment?

Mark one answer
- [ ] **A.** Braking performance
- [ ] **B.** Stability
- [ ] **C.** Acceleration
- [ ] **D.** Suspension preload

123 Why should you wear specialist motorcycle clothing when riding?

Mark one answer

- [ ] **A.** Because the law requires you to do so
- [ ] **B.** Because it looks better than ordinary clothing
- [ ] **C.** Because it gives best protection from the weather
- [ ] **D.** Because it will reduce your insurance

124 When leaving your motorcycle parked, you should always

Mark one answer

- [ ] **A.** remove the battery lead
- [ ] **B.** pull it on to the kerb
- [ ] **C.** use the steering lock
- [ ] **D.** leave the parking light on

125 You are parking your motorcycle. Chaining it to an immovable object will

Mark one answer

- [ ] **A.** be against the law
- [ ] **B.** give extra security
- [ ] **C.** be likely to cause damage
- [ ] **D.** leave the motorcycle unstable

126 You are parking your motorcycle and sidecar on a hill. What is the best way to stop it rolling away?

Mark one answer

- [ ] **A.** Leave it in neutral
- [ ] **B.** Put the rear wheel on the pavement
- [ ] **C.** Leave it in a low gear
- [ ] **D.** Park very close to another vehicle

127 An engine cut-out switch should be used to

Mark one answer

- [ ] **A.** reduce speed in an emergency
- [ ] **B.** prevent the motorcycle being stolen
- [ ] **C.** stop the engine normally
- [ ] **D.** stop the engine in an emergency

128 You enter a road where there are road humps. What should you do?

Mark one answer

- [ ] **A.** Maintain a reduced speed throughout
- [ ] **B.** Accelerate quickly between each one
- [ ] **C.** Always keep to the maximum legal speed
- [ ] **D.** Ride slowly at school times only

129 When should you especially check the engine oil level?

Mark one answer

- [ ] **A.** Before a long journey
- [ ] **B.** When the engine is hot
- [ ] **C.** Early in the morning
- [ ] **D.** Every 6,000 miles

130 You service your own motorcycle. How should you get rid of the old engine oil?

Mark one answer

- A. Take it to a local authority site
- B. Pour it down a drain
- C. Tip it into a hole in the ground
- D. Put it into your dustbin

131 You are leaving your motorcycle unattended on a road. When may you leave the engine running?

Mark one answer

- A. When parked for less than 5 minutes
- B. If the battery is flat
- C. When in a 15mph zone
- D. Not on any occasion

132 What safeguard could you take against fire risk to your motorcycle?

Mark one answer

- A. Keep water levels above maximum
- B. Check out any strong smell of petrol
- C. Avoid riding with a full tank of petrol
- D. Use unleaded petrol

133 Which of these, if allowed to get low, could cause you to crash?

Mark one answer

- A. Anti-freeze level
- B. Brake fluid level
- C. Battery water level
- D. Radiator coolant level

134 Which TWO are badly affected if the tyres are under-inflated?

Mark two answers

- A. Braking
- B. Steering
- C. Changing gear
- D. Parking

135 Motor vehicles can harm the environment. This has resulted in

Mark three answers

- A. air pollution
- B. damage to buildings
- C. less risk to health
- D. improved public transport
- E. less use of electrical vehicles
- F. using up of natural resources

136 Excessive or uneven tyre wear can be caused by faults in which THREE of the following?

Mark three answers

- A. The gearbox
- B. The braking system
- C. The accelerator
- D. The exhaust system
- E. Wheel alignment
- F. The suspension

137 You must NOT sound your horn

Mark one answer

- A. between 10pm and 6am in a built-up area
- B. at any time in a built-up area
- C. between 11.30pm and 7am in a built-up area
- D. between 11.30pm and 6am on any road

138 The pictured vehicle is 'environmentally friendly' because it

Mark three answers

A. reduces noise pollution
B. uses diesel fuel
C. uses electricity
D. uses unleaded fuel
E. reduces parking spaces
F. reduces town traffic

139 Supertrams or Light Rapid Transit (LRT) systems are environmentally friendly because

Mark one answer

A. they use diesel power
B. they use quieter roads
C. they use electric power
D. they do not operate during rush hour

140 'Red routes' in major cities have been introduced to

Mark one answer

A. raise the speed limits
B. help the traffic flow
C. provide better parking
D. allow lorries to load more freely

141 Road humps, chicanes and narrowings are

Mark one answer

A. always at major roadworks
B. used to increase traffic speed
C. at toll-bridge approaches only
D. traffic calming measures

142 The purpose of a catalytic converter is to reduce

Mark one answer

A. fuel consumption
B. the risk of fire
C. toxic exhaust gases
D. engine wear

143 Catalytic converters are fitted to make the

Mark one answer

A. engine produce more power
B. exhaust system easier to replace
C. engine run quietly
D. exhaust fumes cleaner

144 It is essential that tyre pressures are checked regularly. When should this be done?

Mark one answer

A. After any lengthy journey
B. After travelling at high speed
C. When tyres are hot
D. When tyres are cold

145 When should you NOT use your horn in a built-up area?

Mark one answer

A. Between 8pm and 8am
B. Between 9pm and dawn
C. Between dusk and 8am
D. Between 11.30pm and 7am

146 You will use more fuel if your tyres are

Mark one answer

- A. under-inflated
- B. of different makes
- C. over-inflated
- D. new and hardly used

147 How should you dispose of a used battery?

Mark two answers

- A. Take it to a local authority site
- B. Put it in the dustbin
- C. Break it up into pieces
- D. Leave it on waste land
- E. Take it to a garage
- F. Burn it on a fire

148 What is most likely to cause high fuel consumption?

Mark one answer

- A. Poor steering control
- B. Accelerating around bends
- C. Staying in high gears
- D. Harsh braking and accelerating

149 The fluid level in your battery is low. What should you top it up with?

Mark one answer

- A. Battery acid
- B. Distilled water
- C. Engine oil
- D. Engine coolant

150 You need to top up your battery. What level should you fill to?

Mark one answer

- A. The top of the battery
- B. Half-way up the battery
- C. Just below the cell plates
- D. Just above the cell plates

151 You have too much oil in your engine. What could this cause?

Mark one answer

- A. Low oil pressure
- B. Engine overheating
- C. Chain wear
- D. Oil leaks

152 You are parking on a two-way road at night. The speed limit is 40mph. You should park on the

Mark one answer

- A. left with parking lights on
- B. left with no lights on
- C. right with parking lights on
- D. right with dipped headlights on

153 You are parked on the road at night. Where must you use parking lights?

Mark one answer

- A. Where there are continuous white lines in the middle of the road
- B. Where the speed limit exceeds 30mph
- C. Where you are facing oncoming traffic
- D. Where you are near a bus stop

154 Before starting a journey it is wise to plan your route. How can you do this?

Mark one answer

- A. Look at a map
- B. Contact your local garage
- C. Look in your vehicle handbook
- D. Check your vehicle registration document

155 It can help to plan your route before starting a journey. You can do this by contacting

Mark one answer **NI**

- A. your local filling station
- B. a motoring organisation
- C. the Driver Vehicle Licensing Agency
- D. your vehicle manufacturer

156 How can you plan your route before starting a long journey?

Mark one answer

- A. Check your vehicle's workshop manual
- B. Ask your local garage
- C. Use a route planner on the internet
- D. Consult your travel agents

157 Planning your route before setting out can be helpful. How can you do this?

Mark one answer

- A. Look in a motoring magazine
- B. Only visit places you know
- C. Try to travel at busy times
- D. Print or write down the route

158 Why is it a good idea to plan your journey to avoid busy times?

Mark one answer

- A. You will have an easier journey
- B. You will have a more stressful journey
- C. Your journey time will be longer
- D. It will cause more traffic congestion

159 Planning your journey to avoid busy times has a number of advantages. One of these is

Mark one answer

- A. your journey will take longer
- B. you will have a more pleasant journey
- C. you will cause more pollution
- D. your stress level will be greater

160 It is a good idea to plan your journey to avoid busy times. This is because

Mark one answer

- A. your vehicle will use more fuel
- B. you will see less roadworks
- C. it will help to ease congestion
- D. you will travel a much shorter distance

161 By avoiding busy times when travelling

Mark one answer

- A. you are more likely to be held up
- B. your journey time will be longer
- C. you will travel a much shorter distance
- D. you are less likely to be delayed

162 It can help to plan your route before starting a journey. Why should you also plan an alternative route?

Mark one answer

- A. Your original route may be blocked
- B. Your maps may have different scales
- C. You may find you have to pay a congestion charge
- D. Because you may get held up by a tractor

163 As well as planning your route before starting a journey, you should also plan an alternative route. Why is this?

Mark one answer

- **A.** To let another driver overtake
- **B.** Your first route may be blocked
- **C.** To avoid a railway level crossing
- **D.** In case you have to avoid emergency vehicles

164 You are making an appointment and will have to travel a long distance. You should

Mark one answer

- **A.** allow plenty of time for your journey
- **B.** plan to go at busy times
- **C.** avoid all national speed limit roads
- **D.** prevent other drivers from overtaking

165 A loosely adjusted drive chain could

Mark one answer

- **A.** lock the rear wheel
- **B.** make wheels wobble
- **C.** cause a braking fault
- **D.** affect your headlight beam

166 Your motorcycle is NOT fitted with daytime running lights. When MUST you use a dipped headlight during the day?

Mark one answer

- **A.** On country roads
- **B.** In poor visibility
- **C.** Along narrow streets
- **D.** When parking

167 Rapid acceleration and heavy braking can lead to

Mark one answer

- **A.** reduced pollution
- **B.** increased fuel consumption
- **C.** reduced exhaust emissions
- **D.** increased road safety

168 What percentage of all emissions does road transport account for?

Mark one answer

- **A.** 10%
- **B.** 20%
- **C.** 30%
- **D.** 40%

169 You are involved in a crash. To reduce the risk of fire what is the best thing to do?

Mark one answer

- **A.** Keep the engine running
- **B.** Open the choke
- **C.** Turn the fuel tap to reserve
- **D.** Use the engine cut-out switch

170 When riding at night you should

Mark two answers

- **A.** ride with your headlight on
- **B.** wear reflective clothing
- **C.** wear a tinted visor
- **D.** ride in the centre of the road
- **E.** give arm signals

171 Your overall stopping distance will be longer when riding

Mark one answer

- A. at night
- B. in the fog
- C. with a passenger
- D. up a hill

172 Only a fool breaks the two-second rule refers to

Mark one answer

- A. the time recommended when using the choke
- B. the separation distance when riding in good conditions
- C. restarting a stalled engine in busy traffic
- D. the time you should keep your foot down at a junction

173 On a wet road what is the safest way to stop?

Mark one answer

- A. Change gear without braking
- B. Use the back brake only
- C. Use the front brake only
- D. Use both brakes

174 You are riding in heavy rain when your rear wheel skids as you accelerate. To get control again you must

Mark one answer

- A. change down to a lower gear
- B. ease off the throttle
- C. brake to reduce speed
- D. put your feet down

175 It is snowing. Before starting your journey you should

Mark one answer

- A. think if you need to ride at all
- B. try to avoid taking a passenger
- C. plan a route avoiding towns
- D. take a hot drink before setting out

176 Why should you ride with a dipped headlight on in the daytime?

Mark one answer

- A. It helps other road users to see you
- B. It means that you can ride faster
- C. Other vehicles will get out of the way
- D. So that it is already on when it gets dark

177 Motorcyclists are only allowed to use high-intensity rear fog lights when

Mark one answer

- A. a pillion passenger is being carried
- B. they ride a large touring machine
- C. visibility is 100 metres (198 feet) or less
- D. they are riding on the road for the first time

178 You MUST use your headlight

Mark three answers

- A. when riding in a group
- B. at night when street lighting is poor
- C. when carrying a passenger
- D. on motorways during darkness
- E. at times of poor visibility
- F. when parked on an unlit road

179 You are riding in town at night. The roads are wet after rain. The reflections from wet surfaces will

Mark one answer

- A. affect your stopping distance
- B. affect your road holding
- C. make it easy to see unlit objects
- D. make it hard to see unlit objects

180 You are riding through a flood. Which TWO should you do?

Mark two answers

- A. Keep in a high gear and stand up on the footrests
- B. Keep the engine running fast to keep water out of the exhaust
- C. Ride slowly and test your brakes when you are out of the water
- D. Turn your headlight off to avoid any electrical damage

181 You have just ridden through a flood. When clear of the water you should test your

Mark one answer

- A. starter motor
- B. headlight
- C. steering
- D. brakes

182 When going through flood water you should ride

Mark one answer

- A. quickly in a high gear
- B. slowly in a high gear
- C. quickly in a low gear
- D. slowly in a low gear

183 When riding at night you should NOT

Mark one answer

- A. switch on full beam headlights
- B. overtake slower vehicles in front
- C. use dipped beam headlights
- D. use tinted glasses, lenses or visors

184 At a mini-roundabout it is important that a motorcyclist should avoid

Mark one answer

- A. turning right
- B. using signals
- C. taking 'lifesavers'
- D. the painted area

185 Which of the following should you do when riding in fog?

Mark two answers

- A. Keep close to the vehicle in front
- B. Use your dipped headlight
- C. Ride close to the centre of the road
- D. Keep your visor or goggles clear
- E. Keep the vehicle in front in view

186 You are riding on a motorway in a crosswind. You should take extra care when

Mark two answers

- A. approaching service areas
- B. overtaking a large vehicle
- C. riding in slow-moving traffic
- D. approaching an exit
- E. riding in exposed places

187 You are riding in heavy rain. Why should you try to avoid this marked area?

Mark one answer

- A. It is illegal to ride over bus stops
- B. The painted lines may be slippery
- C. Cyclists may be using the bus stop
- D. Only emergency vehicles may drive over bus stops

188 Why should you try to avoid riding over this marked area?

Mark one answer

- A. It is illegal to ride over bus stops
- B. It will alter your machine's centre of gravity
- C. Pedestrians may be waiting at the bus stop
- D. A bus may have left patches of oil

189 When riding at night you should

Mark one answer

- A. wear reflective clothing
- B. wear a tinted visor
- C. ride in the middle of the road
- D. always give arm signals

190 When riding in extremely cold conditions what can you do to keep warm?

Mark one answer

- A. Stay close to the vehicles in front
- B. Wear suitable clothing
- C. Lie flat on the tank
- D. Put one hand on the exhaust pipe

191 You are riding at night. To be seen more easily you should

Mark two answers

- A. ride with your headlight on dipped beam
- B. wear reflective clothing
- C. keep the motorcycle clean
- D. stay well out to the right
- E. wear waterproof clothing

192 Your overall stopping distance will be much longer when riding

Mark one answer

- A. in the rain
- B. in fog
- C. at night
- D. in strong winds

193 The road surface is very important to motorcyclists. Which FOUR of these are more likely to reduce the stability of your motorcycle?

Mark four answers

- A. Potholes
- B. Drain covers
- C. Concrete
- D. Oil patches
- E. Tarmac
- F. Loose gravel

194 You are riding in very hot weather. What are TWO effects that melting tar has on the control of your motorcycle?

Mark two answers

- A. It can make the surface slippery
- B. It can reduce tyre grip
- C. It can reduce stopping distances
- D. It can improve braking efficiency

195 Your overall stopping distance comprises thinking and braking distance. You are on a good, dry road surface with good brakes and tyres. What is the typical BRAKING distance at 50mph?

Mark one answer

- A. 14 metres (46 feet)
- B. 24 metres (79 feet)
- C. 38 metres (125 feet)
- D. 55 metres (180 feet)

196 You are riding past queuing traffic. Why should you be more cautious when approaching this road marking?

KEEP CLEAR

Mark one answer

- A. Lorries will be unloading here
- B. Schoolchildren will be crossing here
- C. Pedestrians will be standing in the road
- D. Traffic could be emerging and may not see you

197 What can cause your tyres to skid and lose their grip on the road surface?

Mark one answer

- A. Giving hand signals
- B. Riding one handed
- C. Looking over your shoulder
- D. Heavy braking

198 You are riding at speed through surface water. A thin film of water has built up between your tyres and the road surface. To keep control what should you do?

Mark one answer

- A. Turn the steering quickly
- B. Use the rear brake gently
- C. Use both brakes gently
- D. Ease off the throttle

199 When riding in heavy rain a film of water can build up between your tyres and the road surface. This may result in loss of control. What can you do to avoid this happening?

Mark one answer

- A. Keep your speed down
- B. Increase your tyre pressures
- C. Decrease your tyre pressures
- D. Keep trying your brakes

200 When riding in heavy rain a film of water can build up between your tyres and the road. This is known as aquaplaning. What should you do to keep control?

Mark one answer
- A. Use your rear brakes gently
- B. Steer to the crown of the road
- C. Ease off the throttle smoothly
- D. Change up into a higher gear

201 After riding through deep water you notice your scooter brakes do not work properly. What would be the best way to dry them out?

Mark one answer
- A. Ride slowly, braking lightly
- B. Ride quickly, braking harshly
- C. Stop and dry them with a cloth
- D. Stop and wait for a few minutes

202 You have to ride in foggy weather. You should

Mark two answers
- A. stay close to the centre of the road
- B. switch only your sidelights on
- C. switch on your dipped headlights
- D. be aware of others not using their headlights
- E. always ride in the gutter to see the kerb

203 Braking distances on ice can be

Mark one answer
- A. twice the normal distance
- B. five times the normal distance
- C. seven times the normal distance
- D. ten times the normal distance

204 Freezing conditions will affect the distance it takes you to come to a stop. You should expect stopping distances to increase by up to

Mark one answer
- A. two times
- B. three times
- C. five times
- D. ten times

205 In very hot weather the road surface can become soft. Which TWO of the following will be most affected?

Mark two answers
- A. The suspension
- B. The grip of the tyres
- C. The braking
- D. The exhaust

206 Where are you most likely to be affected by a side wind?

Mark one answer
- A. On a narrow country lane
- B. On an open stretch of road
- C. On a busy stretch of road
- D. On a long, straight road

207 In windy conditions you need to take extra care when

Mark one answer
- A. using the brakes
- B. making a hill start
- C. turning into a narrow road
- D. passing pedal cyclists

208 In good conditions, what is the typical stopping distance at 70mph?

Mark one answer

- **A.** 53 metres (175 feet)
- **B.** 60 metres (197 feet)
- **C.** 73 metres (240 feet)
- **D.** 96 metres (185 feet)

209 What is the shortest overall stopping distance on a dry road at 60mph?

Mark one answer

- **A.** 53 metres (175 feet)
- **B.** 58 metres (190 feet)
- **C.** 73 metres (240 feet)
- **D.** 96 metres (185 feet)

210 You are following a vehicle at a safe distance on a wet road. Another driver overtakes you and pulls into the gap you have left. What should you do?

Mark one answer

- **A.** Flash your headlights as a warning
- **B.** Try to overtake safely as soon as you can
- **C.** Drop back to regain a safe distance
- **D.** Stay close to the other vehicle until it moves on

211 When approaching a right-hand bend you should keep well to the left. Why is this?

Mark one answer

- **A.** To improve your view of the road
- **B.** To overcome the effect of the road's slope
- **C.** To let faster traffic from behind overtake
- **D.** To be positioned safely if you skid

212 You have just gone through deep water. To dry off the brakes you should

Mark one answer

- **A.** accelerate and keep to a high speed for a short time
- **B.** go slowly while gently applying the brakes
- **C.** avoid using the brakes at all for a few miles
- **D.** stop for at least an hour to allow them time to dry

213 You are travelling at 50mph on a good, dry road. What is your typical overall stopping distance?

Mark one answer

- **A.** 36 metres (120 feet)
- **B.** 53 metres (175 feet)
- **C.** 75 metres (245 feet)
- **D.** 96 metres (185 feet)

214 Overall stopping distance is made up of thinking and braking distance. You are on a good, dry road surface with good brakes and tyres. What is the typical BRAKING distance from 50mph?

Mark one answer

- **A.** 14 metres (46 feet)
- **B.** 24 metres (80 feet)
- **C.** 38 metres (125 feet)
- **D.** 55 metres (180 feet)

215 You are on a good, dry road surface. Your brakes and tyres are good. What is the typical overall STOPPING distance at 40mph?

Mark one answer

- **A.** 23 metres (75 feet)
- **B.** 36 metres (120 feet)
- **C.** 53 metres (175 feet)
- **D.** 96 metres (315 feet)

216 What should you do when overtaking a motorcyclist in strong winds?

Mark one answer

- **A.** Pass close
- **B.** Pass quickly
- **C.** Pass wide
- **D.** Pass immediately

217 You are overtaking a motorcyclist in strong winds? What should you do?

Mark one answer

- **A.** Allow extra room
- **B.** Give a thank you wave
- **C.** Move back early
- **D.** Sound your horn

218 In heavy motorway traffic the vehicle behind you is following too closely. How can you lower the risk of a collision?

Mark one answer

- **A.** Increase your distance from the vehicle in front
- **B.** Operate the brakes sharply
- **C.** Switch on your hazard lights
- **D.** Move onto the hard shoulder and stop

219 You are following other vehicles in fog. You have your lights on. What else can you do to reduce the chances of being in a collision?

Mark one answer

- **A.** Keep close to the vehicle in front
- **B.** Use your main beam instead of dipped headlights
- **C.** Keep up with the faster vehicles
- **D.** Reduce your speed and increase the gap in front

220 To avoid a collision when entering a contraflow system, you should

Mark three answers

- **A.** reduce speed in good time
- **B.** switch lanes at any time to make progress
- **C.** choose an appropriate lane in good time
- **D.** keep the correct separation distance
- **E.** increase speed to pass through quickly
- **F.** follow other motorists closely to avoid long queues

221 You get cold and wet when riding. Which TWO are likely to happen?

Mark two answers
- [ ] **A.** You may lose concentration
- [ ] **B.** You may slide off the seat
- [ ] **C.** Your visor may freeze up
- [ ] **D.** Your reaction times may be slower
- [ ] **E.** Your helmet may loosen

222 You are riding up to a zebra crossing. You intend to stop for waiting pedestrians. How could you let them know you are stopping?

Mark one answer
- [ ] **A.** By signalling with your left arm
- [ ] **B.** By waving them across
- [ ] **C.** By flashing your headlight
- [ ] **D.** By signalling with your right arm

223 You are about to ride home. You cannot find the glasses you need to wear. You should

Mark one answer
- [ ] **A.** ride home slowly, keeping to quiet roads
- [ ] **B.** borrow a friend's glasses and use those
- [ ] **C.** ride home at night, so that the lights will help you
- [ ] **D.** find a way of getting home without riding

224 Which THREE of these are likely effects of drinking alcohol?

Mark three answers
- [ ] **A.** Reduced co-ordination
- [ ] **B.** Increased confidence
- [ ] **C.** Poor judgement
- [ ] **D.** Increased concentration
- [ ] **E.** Faster reactions
- [ ] **F.** Colour blindness

225 You find that you need glasses to read vehicle number plates at the required distance. When MUST you wear them?

Mark one answer
- [ ] **A.** Only in bad weather conditions
- [ ] **B.** At all times when riding
- [ ] **C.** Only when you think it necessary
- [ ] **D.** Only in bad light or at night time

226 Drinking any amount of alcohol is likely to

Mark three answers
- [ ] **A.** slow down your reactions to hazards
- [ ] **B.** increase the speed of your reactions
- [ ] **C.** worsen your judgement of speed
- [ ] **D.** improve your awareness of danger
- [ ] **E.** give a false sense of confidence

227 Which of the following types of glasses should NOT be worn when riding at night?

Mark one answer
- [ ] **A.** Half-moon
- [ ] **B.** Round
- [ ] **C.** Bi-focal
- [ ] **D.** Tinted

228 You are not sure if your cough medicine will affect you. What TWO things should you do?

Mark two answers
- [ ] **A.** Ask your doctor
- [ ] **B.** Check the medicine label
- [ ] **C.** Ride if you feel alright
- [ ] **D.** Ask a friend or relative for advice

229 For which of these may you use hazard warning lights?

Mark one answer

- [ ] **A.** When riding on a motorway to warn traffic behind of a hazard ahead
- [ ] **B.** When you are double parked on a two-way road
- [ ] **C.** When your direction indicators are not working
- [ ] **D.** When warning oncoming traffic that you intend to stop

230 When should you use hazard warning lights?

Mark one answer

- [ ] **A.** When you are double parked on a two-way road
- [ ] **B.** When your direction indicators are not working
- [ ] **C.** When warning oncoming traffic that you intend to stop
- [ ] **D.** When your motorcycle has broken down and is causing an obstruction

231 Why should you check over your shoulder before turning right into a side road?

Mark one answer

- [ ] **A.** To make sure the side road is clear
- [ ] **B.** To check for emerging traffic
- [ ] **C.** To check for overtaking vehicles
- [ ] **D.** To confirm your intention to turn

232 When riding how can you help to reduce the risk of hearing damage?

Mark one answer

- [ ] **A.** Wearing goggles
- [ ] **B.** Using ear plugs
- [ ] **C.** Wearing a scarf
- [ ] **D.** Keeping the visor up

233 It is a very hot day. What would you expect to find?

Mark one answer

- [ ] **A.** Mud on the road
- [ ] **B.** A soft road surface
- [ ] **C.** Roadworks ahead
- [ ] **D.** Banks of fog

234 You see this road marking in between queuing traffic. What should you look out for?

Mark one answer

- [ ] **A.** Overhanging trees
- [ ] **B.** Roadworks
- [ ] **C.** Traffic wardens
- [ ] **D.** Traffic emerging

KEEP CLEAR

235 When riding long distances at speed, noise can cause fatigue. What can you do to help reduce this?

Mark one answer

- [ ] **A.** Vary your speed
- [ ] **B.** Wear ear plugs
- [ ] **C.** Use an open-face helmet
- [ ] **D.** Ride in an upright position

236 Why should you wear ear plugs when riding a motorcycle?

Mark one answer

- [ ] **A.** To help to prevent ear damage
- [ ] **B.** To make you less aware of traffic
- [ ] **C.** To help to keep you warm
- [ ] **D.** To make your helmet fit better

237
You are going out to a social event and alcohol will be available. You will be riding your motorcycle shortly afterwards. What is the safest thing to do?

Mark one answer
- A. Stay just below the legal limit
- B. Have soft drinks and alcohol in turn
- C. Don't go beyond the legal limit
- D. Stick to non-alcoholic drinks

238
You are convicted of riding after drinking too much alcohol. How could this affect your insurance?

Mark one answer
- A. Your insurance may become invalid
- B. The amount of excess you pay will be reduced
- C. You will only be able to get third party cover
- D. Cover will only be given for riding smaller motorcycles

239
You see this sign on the rear of a slow-moving lorry that you want to pass. It is travelling in the middle lane of a three-lane motorway. You should

Mark one answer
- A. cautiously approach the lorry then pass on either side
- B. follow the lorry until you can leave the motorway
- C. wait on the hard shoulder until the lorry has stopped
- D. approach with care and keep to the left of the lorry

240
Where would you expect to see these markers?

Mark two answers
- A. On a motorway sign
- B. At the entrance to a narrow bridge
- C. On a large goods vehicle
- D. On a builder's skip placed on the road

241
What does this signal from a police officer mean to oncoming traffic?

Mark one answer
- A. Go ahead
- B. Stop
- C. Turn left
- D. Turn right

242
What is the main hazard shown in this picture?

Mark one answer

- **A.** Vehicles turning right
- **B.** Vehicles doing U-turns
- **C.** The cyclist crossing the road
- **D.** Parked cars around the corner

243
Which road user has caused a hazard?

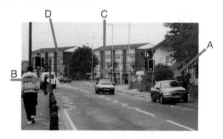

Mark one answer

- **A.** The parked car (arrowed A)
- **B.** The pedestrian waiting to cross (arrowed B)
- **C.** The moving car (arrowed C)
- **D.** The car turning (arrowed D)

244
What should the driver of the car approaching the crossing do?

Mark one answer

- **A.** Continue at the same speed
- **B.** Sound the horn
- **C.** Drive through quickly
- **D.** Slow down and get ready to stop

245
What THREE things should the driver of the grey car (arrowed) be especially aware of?

Mark three answers

- **A.** Pedestrians stepping out between cars
- **B.** Other cars behind the grey car
- **C.** Doors opening on parked cars
- **D.** The bumpy road surface
- **E.** Cars leaving parking spaces
- **F.** Empty parking spaces

246 You think the driver of the vehicle in front has forgotten to cancel their right indicator. You should

Mark one answer
- A. flash your lights to alert the driver
- B. sound your horn before overtaking
- C. overtake on the left if there is room
- D. stay behind and not overtake

247 What is the main hazard the driver of the red car (arrowed) should be aware of?

Mark one answer
- A. Glare from the sun may affect the driver's vision
- B. The black car may stop suddenly
- C. The bus may move out into the road
- D. Oncoming vehicles will assume the driver is turning right

248 You see this sign ahead. You should expect the road to

Mark one answer
- A. go steeply uphill
- B. go steeply downhill
- C. bend sharply to the left
- D. bend sharply to the right

249 You are approaching this cyclist. You should

Mark one answer
- A. overtake before the cyclist gets to the junction
- B. flash your headlights at the cyclist
- C. slow down and allow the cyclist to turn
- D. overtake the cyclist on the left-hand side

250 Why must you take extra care when turning right at this junction?

Mark one answer
- A. Road surface is poor
- B. Footpaths are narrow
- C. Road markings are faint
- D. There is reduced visibility

251 This yellow sign on a vehicle indicates this is

Mark one answer

- [ ] **A.** a broken-down vehicle
- [ ] **B.** a school bus
- [ ] **C.** an ice-cream van
- [ ] **D.** a private ambulance

252 When approaching this bridge you should give way to

Mark one answer

- [ ] **A.** bicycles
- [ ] **B.** buses
- [ ] **C.** motorcycles
- [ ] **D.** cars

253 What type of vehicle could you expect to meet in the middle of the road?

Mark one answer

- [ ] **A.** Lorry
- [ ] **B.** Bicycle
- [ ] **C.** Car
- [ ] **D.** Motorcycle

254 At this blind junction you must stop

Mark one answer

- [ ] **A.** behind the line, then edge forward to see clearly
- [ ] **B.** beyond the line at a point where you can see clearly
- [ ] **C.** only if there is traffic on the main road
- [ ] **D.** only if you are turning to the right

255 A driver pulls out of a side road in front of you. You have to brake hard. You should

Mark one answer

- [ ] **A.** ignore the error and stay calm
- [ ] **B.** flash your lights to show your annoyance
- [ ] **C.** sound your horn to show your annoyance
- [ ] **D.** overtake as soon as possible

256 An elderly person's driving ability could be affected because they may be unable to

Mark one answer

- [ ] **A.** obtain car insurance
- [ ] **B.** understand road signs
- [ ] **C.** react very quickly
- [ ] **D.** give signals correctly

257 You have just passed these warning lights. What hazard would you expect to see next?

Mark one answer

- **A.** A level crossing with no barrier
- **B.** An ambulance station
- **C.** A school crossing patrol
- **D.** An opening bridge

258 Why should you be especially cautious when going past this stationary bus?

Mark two answers

- **A.** There is traffic approaching in the distance
- **B.** The driver may open the door
- **C.** It may suddenly move off
- **D.** People may cross the road in front of it
- **E.** There are bicycles parked on the pavement

259 In areas where there are 'traffic calming' measures you should

Mark one answer

- **A.** travel at a reduced speed
- **B.** always travel at the speed limit
- **C.** position in the centre of the road
- **D.** only slow down if pedestrians are near

260 You are planning a long journey. Do you need to plan rest stops?

Mark one answer

- **A.** Yes, you should plan to stop every half an hour
- **B.** Yes, regular stops help concentration
- **C.** No, you will be less tired if you get there as soon as possible
- **D.** No, only fuel stops will be needed

261 A driver does something that upsets you. You should

Mark one answer

- **A.** try not to react
- **B.** let them know how you feel
- **C.** flash your headlights several times
- **D.** sound your horn

262 Some two-way roads are divided into three lanes. Why are these particularly dangerous?

Mark one answer

- **A.** Traffic in both directions can use the middle lane to overtake
- **B.** Traffic can travel faster in poor weather conditions
- **C.** Traffic can overtake on the left
- **D.** Traffic uses the middle lane for emergencies only

263
The red lights are flashing. What should you do when approaching this level crossing?

Mark one answer
- **A.** Go through quickly
- **B.** Go through carefully
- **C.** Stop before the barrier
- **D.** Switch on hazard warning lights

264
What TWO main hazards should you be aware of when going along this street?

Mark two answers
- **A.** Glare from the sun
- **B.** Car doors opening suddenly
- **C.** Lack of road markings
- **D.** The headlights on parked cars being switched on
- **E.** Large goods vehicles
- **F.** Children running out from between vehicles

265
What is the main hazard you should be aware of when following this cyclist?

Mark one answer
- **A.** The cyclist may move to the left and dismount
- **B.** The cyclist may swerve out into the road
- **C.** The contents of the cyclist's carrier may fall on to the road
- **D.** The cyclist may wish to turn right at the end of the road

266
When approaching this hazard why should you slow down?

Mark two answers
- **A.** Because of the bend
- **B.** Because it's hard to see to the right
- **C.** Because of approaching traffic
- **D.** Because of animals crossing
- **E.** Because of the level crossing

267 A driver's behaviour has upset you. It may help if you

Mark one answer
- A. stop and take a break
- B. shout abusive language
- C. gesture to them with your hand
- D. follow their car, flashing your headlights

268 You are on a dual carriageway. Ahead you see a vehicle with an amber flashing light. What will this be?

Mark one answer
- A. An ambulance
- B. A fire engine
- C. A doctor on call
- D. A disabled person's vehicle

269 You are approaching crossroads. The traffic lights have failed. What should you do?

Mark one answer
- A. Brake and stop only for large vehicles
- B. Brake sharply to a stop before looking
- C. Be prepared to brake sharply to a stop
- D. Be prepared to stop for any traffic

270 Why are place names painted on the road surface?

Mark one answer
- A. To restrict the flow of traffic
- B. To warn you of oncoming traffic
- C. To enable you to change lanes early
- D. To prevent you changing lanes

271 What should the driver of the red car (arrowed) do?

Mark one answer
- A. Wave the pedestrians who are waiting to cross
- B. Wait for the pedestrian in the road to cross
- C. Quickly drive behind the pedestrian in the road
- D. Tell the pedestrian in the road she should not have crossed

272 You are following a slower-moving vehicle on a narrow country road. There is a junction just ahead on the right. What should you do?

Mark one answer
- A. Overtake after checking your mirrors and signalling
- B. Stay behind until you are past the junction
- C. Accelerate quickly to pass before the junction
- D. Slow down and prepare to overtake on the left

273 What should you do as you approach this overhead bridge?

Mark one answer

- [ ] **A.** Move out to the centre of the road before going through
- [ ] **B.** Find another route, this is only for high vehicles
- [ ] **C.** Be prepared to give way to large vehicles in the middle of the road
- [ ] **D.** Move across to the right-hand side before going through

274 Why are mirrors often slightly curved (convex)?

Mark one answer

- [ ] **A.** They give a wider field of vision
- [ ] **B.** They totally cover blind spots
- [ ] **C.** They make it easier to judge the speed of following traffic
- [ ] **D.** They make following traffic look bigger

275 Which THREE result from drinking alcohol?

Mark three answers

- [ ] **A.** Less control
- [ ] **B.** A false sense of confidence
- [ ] **C.** Faster reactions
- [ ] **D.** Poor judgement of speed
- [ ] **E.** Greater awareness of danger

276 Overtaking is a major cause of collisions. In which THREE of these situations should you NOT overtake?

Mark three answers

- [ ] **A.** If you are turning left shortly afterwards
- [ ] **B.** When you are in a one-way street
- [ ] **C.** When you are approaching a junction
- [ ] **D.** If you are travelling up a long hill
- [ ] **E.** When your view ahead is blocked

277 You should not ride too closely behind a lorry because

Mark one answer

- **A.** you will breathe in the lorry's exhaust fumes
- **B.** wind from the lorry will slow you down
- **C.** drivers behind you may not be able to see you
- **D.** it will reduce your view ahead

278 You are riding on a country lane. You see cattle on the road. You should

Mark three answers

- **A.** slow down
- **B.** stop if necessary
- **C.** give plenty of room
- **D.** rev your engine
- **E.** sound your horn
- **F.** ride up close behind them

279 A learner driver has begun to emerge into your path from a side road on the left. You should

Mark one answer

- **A.** be ready to slow down and stop
- **B.** let them emerge then ride close behind
- **C.** turn into the side road
- **D.** brake hard, then wave them out

280 The vehicle ahead is being driven by a learner. You should

Mark one answer

- **A.** keep calm and be patient
- **B.** ride up close behind
- **C.** put your headlight on full beam
- **D.** sound your horn and overtake

281 Why is it vital for a rider to make a 'lifesaver' check before turning right?

Mark one answer

- **A.** To check for any overtaking traffic
- **B.** To confirm that they are about to turn
- **C.** To make sure the side road is clear
- **D.** To check that the rear indicator is flashing

282 You are riding in fast-flowing traffic. The vehicle behind is following too closely. You should

Mark one answer

- **A.** slow down gradually to increase the gap in front of you
- **B.** slow down as quickly as possible by braking
- **C.** accelerate to get away from the vehicle behind you
- **D.** apply the brakes sharply to warn the driver behind

283 You are riding towards a zebra crossing. Waiting to cross is a person in a wheelchair. You should

Mark one answer

- **A.** continue on your way
- **B.** wave to the person to cross
- **C.** wave to the person to wait
- **D.** be prepared to stop

284 Why should you allow extra room when overtaking another motorcyclist on a windy day?

Mark one answer

- A. The rider may turn off suddenly to get out of the wind
- B. The rider may be blown across in front of you
- C. The rider may stop suddenly
- D. The rider may be travelling faster than normal

285 You have stopped at a pelican crossing. A disabled person is crossing slowly in front of you. The lights have now changed to green. You should

Mark two answers

- A. allow the person to cross
- B. ride in front of the person
- C. ride behind the person
- D. sound your horn
- E. be patient
- F. edge forward slowly

286 Where should you take particular care to look out for other motorcyclists and cyclists?

Mark one answer

- A. On dual carriageways
- B. At junctions
- C. At zebra crossings
- D. On one-way streets

287 What is a main cause of road traffic incidents among young and new motorcyclists?

Mark one answer

- A. Using borrowed equipment
- B. Lack of experience and judgement
- C. Riding in bad weather conditions
- D. Riding on country roads

288 Which of the following is applicable to young motorcyclists?

Mark one answer

- A. They are normally better than experienced riders
- B. They are usually less likely to have a crash
- C. They are often over-confident of their own ability
- D. They are more likely to get cheaper insurance

289 You are about to overtake horse riders. Which TWO of the following could scare the horses?

Mark two answers

- A. Sounding your horn
- B. Giving arm signals
- C. Riding slowly
- D. Revving your engine

290 The road outside this school is marked with yellow zigzag lines. What do these lines mean?

Mark one answer
- [ ] **A.** You may park on the lines when dropping off schoolchildren
- [ ] **B.** You may park on the lines when picking up schoolchildren
- [ ] **C.** You should not wait or park your motorcycle here
- [ ] **D.** You must stay with your motorcycle if you park here

291 Which sign means that there may be people walking along the road?

Mark one answer
- [ ] **A.**
- [ ] **B.**
- [ ] **C.**
- [ ] **D.**

292 You are turning left at a junction. Pedestrians have started to cross the road. You should

Mark one answer
- [ ] **A.** go on, giving them plenty of room
- [ ] **B.** stop and wave at them to cross
- [ ] **C.** blow your horn and proceed
- [ ] **D.** give way to them

293 You are turning left from a main road into a side road. People are already crossing the road into which you are turning. You should

Mark one answer
- [ ] **A.** continue, as it is your right of way
- [ ] **B.** signal to them to continue crossing
- [ ] **C.** wait and allow them to cross
- [ ] **D.** sound your horn to warn them of your presence

294
You are at a road junction, turning into a minor road. There are pedestrians crossing the minor road. You should

Mark one answer

- [ ] **A.** stop and wave the pedestrians across
- [ ] **B.** sound your horn to let the pedestrians know that you are there
- [ ] **C.** give way to the pedestrians who are already crossing
- [ ] **D.** carry on; the pedestrians should give way to you

295
You are turning left into a side road. What hazards should you be especially aware of?

Mark one answer

- [ ] **A.** One-way street
- [ ] **B.** Pedestrians
- [ ] **C.** Traffic congestion
- [ ] **D.** Parked vehicles

296
You intend to turn right into a side road. Just before turning you should check for motorcyclists who might be

Mark one answer

- [ ] **A.** overtaking on your left
- [ ] **B.** following you closely
- [ ] **C.** emerging from the side road
- [ ] **D.** overtaking on your right

297
A toucan crossing is different from other crossings because

Mark one answer

- [ ] **A.** moped riders can use it
- [ ] **B.** it is controlled by a traffic warden
- [ ] **C.** it is controlled by two flashing lights
- [ ] **D.** cyclists can use it

298
At toucan crossings

Mark one answer

- [ ] **A.** you only stop if someone is waiting to cross
- [ ] **B.** cyclists are not permitted
- [ ] **C.** there is a continuously flashing amber beacon
- [ ] **D.** pedestrians and cyclists may cross

299
What does this sign tell you?

Mark one answer

- [ ] **A.** No cycling
- [ ] **B.** Cycle route ahead
- [ ] **C.** Cycle parking only
- [ ] **D.** End of cycle route

300
How will a school crossing patrol signal you to stop?

Mark one answer

- [ ] **A.** By pointing to children on the opposite pavement
- [ ] **B.** By displaying a red light
- [ ] **C.** By displaying a stop sign
- [ ] **D.** By giving you an arm signal

301 Where would you see this sign?

Mark one answer

- **A.** In the window of a car taking children to school
- **B.** At the side of the road
- **C.** At playground areas
- **D.** On the rear of a school bus or coach

302 Which sign tells you that pedestrians may be walking in the road as there is no pavement?

Mark one answer

A.   **B.**

C.   **D.**

303 What does this sign mean?

Mark one answer

- **A.** No route for pedestrians and cyclists
- **B.** A route for pedestrians only
- **C.** A route for cyclists only
- **D.** A route for pedestrians and cyclists

304 You see a pedestrian with a white stick and red band. This means that the person is

Mark one answer

- **A.** physically disabled
- **B.** deaf only
- **C.** blind only
- **D.** deaf and blind

305 What action would you take when elderly people are crossing the road?

Mark one answer

- **A.** Wave them across so they know that you have seen them
- **B.** Be patient and allow them to cross in their own time
- **C.** Rev the engine to let them know that you are waiting
- **D.** Tap the horn in case they are hard of hearing

306 You see two elderly pedestrians about to cross the road ahead. You should

Mark one answer

- **A.** expect them to wait for you to pass
- **B.** speed up to get past them quickly
- **C.** stop and wave them across the road
- **D.** be careful, they may misjudge your speed

307 What does this sign mean?

Mark one answer

- A. Contraflow pedal cycle lane
- B. With-flow pedal cycle lane
- C. Pedal cycles and buses only
- D. No pedal cycles or buses

308 You are coming up to a roundabout. A cyclist is signalling to turn right. What should you do?

Mark one answer

- A. Overtake on the right
- B. Give a horn warning
- C. Signal the cyclist to move across
- D. Give the cyclist plenty of room

309 You are approaching this roundabout and see the cyclist signal right. Why is the cyclist keeping to the left?

Mark one answer

- A. It is a quicker route for the cyclist
- B. The cyclist is going to turn left instead
- C. The cyclist thinks *The Highway Code* does not apply to bicycles
- D. The cyclist is slower and more vulnerable

310 When you are overtaking a cyclist you should leave as much room as you would give to a car. What is the main reason for this?

Mark one answer

- A. The cyclist might speed up
- B. The cyclist might get off the bike
- C. The cyclist might swerve
- D. The cyclist might have to make a left turn

311 Which TWO should you allow extra room when overtaking?

Mark two answers

- A. Motorcycles
- B. Tractors
- C. Bicycles
- D. Road-sweeping vehicles

312 Why should you look particularly for motorcyclists and cyclists at junctions?

Mark one answer

- A. They may want to turn into the side road
- B. They may slow down to let you turn
- C. They are harder to see
- D. They might not see you turn

313 You are waiting to come out of a side road. Why should you watch carefully for motorcycles?

Mark one answer

- A. Motorcycles are usually faster than cars
- B. Police patrols often use motorcycles
- C. Motorcycles are small and hard to see
- D. Motorcycles have right of way

314 In daylight, an approaching motorcyclist is using a dipped headlight. Why?

Mark one answer

- [ ] **A.** So that the rider can be seen more easily
- [ ] **B.** To stop the battery overcharging
- [ ] **C.** To improve the rider's vision
- [ ] **D.** The rider is inviting you to proceed

315 Motorcyclists should wear bright clothing mainly because

Mark one answer

- [ ] **A.** they must do so by law
- [ ] **B.** it helps keep them cool in summer
- [ ] **C.** the colours are popular
- [ ] **D.** drivers often do not see them

316 There is a slow-moving motorcyclist ahead of you. You are unsure what the rider is going to do. You should

Mark one answer

- [ ] **A.** pass on the left
- [ ] **B.** pass on the right
- [ ] **C.** stay behind
- [ ] **D.** move closer

317 Motorcyclists will often look round over their right shoulder just before turning right. This is because

Mark one answer

- [ ] **A.** they need to listen for following traffic
- [ ] **B.** motorcycles do not have mirrors
- [ ] **C.** looking around helps them balance as they turn
- [ ] **D.** they need to check for traffic in their blind area

318 At road junctions which of the following are most vulnerable?

Mark three answers

- [ ] **A.** Cyclists
- [ ] **B.** Motorcyclists
- [ ] **C.** Pedestrians
- [ ] **D.** Car drivers
- [ ] **E.** Lorry drivers

319 Motorcyclists are particularly vulnerable

Mark one answer

- [ ] **A.** when moving off
- [ ] **B.** on dual carriageways
- [ ] **C.** when approaching junctions
- [ ] **D.** on motorways

320 You notice horse riders in front. What should you do FIRST?

Mark one answer

- [ ] **A.** Pull out to the middle of the road
- [ ] **B.** Slow down and be ready to stop
- [ ] **C.** Accelerate around them
- [ ] **D.** Signal right

321
You are approaching a roundabout. There are horses just ahead of you. You should

Mark two answers

- A. be prepared to stop
- B. treat them like any other vehicle
- C. give them plenty of room
- D. accelerate past as quickly as possible
- E. sound your horn as a warning

322
Which THREE should you do when passing sheep on a road?

Mark three answers

- A. Allow plenty of room
- B. Go very slowly
- C. Pass quickly but quietly
- D. Be ready to stop
- E. Briefly sound your horn

323
At night you see a pedestrian wearing reflective clothing and carrying a bright red light. What does this mean?

Mark one answer

- A. You are approaching road works
- B. You are approaching an organised walk
- C. You are approaching a slow-moving vehicle
- D. You are approaching a traffic danger spot

324
As you approach a pelican crossing the lights change to green. Elderly people are halfway across. You should

Mark one answer

- A. wave them to cross as quickly as they can
- B. rev your engine to make them hurry
- C. flash your lights in case they have not heard you
- D. wait because they will take longer to cross

325
There are flashing amber lights under a school warning sign. What action should you take?

Mark one answer

- A. Reduce speed until you are clear of the area
- B. Keep up your speed and sound the horn
- C. Increase your speed to clear the area quickly
- D. Wait at the lights until they change to green

326
You are approaching this crossing. You should

Mark one answer

- A. prepare to slow down and stop
- B. stop and wave the pedestrians across
- C. speed up and pass by quickly
- D. continue unless the pedestrians step out

327 You see a pedestrian with a dog. The dog has a yellow or burgundy coat. This especially warns you that the pedestrian is

Mark one answer

A. elderly
B. dog training
C. colour blind
D. deaf

328 These road markings must be kept clear to allow

W-SCHOOL KEEP CLEAR-W

Mark one answer

A. schoolchildren to be dropped off
B. for teachers to park
C. schoolchildren to be picked up
D. a clear view of the crossing area

329 You must not stop on these road markings because you may obstruct

W-SCHOOL KEEP CLEAR-W

Mark one answer

A. children's view of the crossing area
B. teachers' access to the school
C. delivery vehicles' access to the school
D. emergency vehicles' access to the school

330 The left-hand pavement is closed due to street repairs. What should you do?

Mark one answer

A. Watch out for pedestrians walking in the road
B. Use your right-hand mirror more often
C. Speed up to get past the road works quicker
D. Position close to the left-hand kerb

331 Where would you see this sign?

Mark one answer

A. Near a school crossing
B. At a playground entrance
C. On a school bus
D. At a 'pedestrians only' area

332 You are following a motorcyclist on an uneven road. You should

Mark one answer

A. allow less room so you can be seen in their mirrors
B. overtake immediately
C. allow extra room in case they swerve to avoid potholes
D. allow the same room as normal because road surfaces do not affect motorcyclists

333
You are following two cyclists. They approach a roundabout in the left-hand lane. In which direction should you expect the cyclists to go?

Mark one answer

- A. Left
- B. Right
- C. Any direction
- D. Straight ahead

334
You are travelling behind a moped. You want to turn left just ahead. You should

Mark one answer

- A. overtake the moped before the junction
- B. pull alongside the moped and stay level until just before the junction
- C. sound your horn as a warning and pull in front of the moped
- D. stay behind until the moped has passed the junction

335
You see a horse rider as you approach a roundabout. They are signalling right but keeping well to the left. You should

Mark one answer

- A. proceed as normal
- B. keep close to them
- C. cut in front of them
- D. stay well back

336
How would you react to drivers who appear to be inexperienced?

Mark one answer

- A. Sound your horn to warn them of your presence
- B. Be patient and prepare for them to react more slowly
- C. Flash your headlights to indicate that it is safe for them to proceed
- D. Overtake them as soon as possible

337
You are following a learner driver who stalls at a junction. You should

Mark one answer

- A. be patient as you expect them to make mistakes
- B. stay very close behind and flash your headlights
- C. start to rev your engine if they take too long to restart
- D. immediately steer around them and drive on

338
You are on a country road. What should you expect to see coming towards you on YOUR side of the road?

Mark one answer

- A. Motorcycles
- B. Bicycles
- C. Pedestrians
- D. Horse riders

339

You are turning left into a side road. Pedestrians are crossing the road near the junction. You must

Mark one answer
- A. wave them on
- B. sound your horn
- C. switch on your hazard lights
- D. wait for them to cross

340

You are following a car driven by an elderly driver. You should

Mark one answer
- A. expect the driver to drive badly
- B. flash your lights and overtake
- C. be aware that the driver's reactions may not be as fast as yours
- D. stay very close behind but be careful

341

You are following a cyclist. You wish to turn left just ahead. You should

Mark one answer
- A. overtake the cyclist before the junction
- B. pull alongside the cyclist and stay level until after the junction
- C. hold back until the cyclist has passed the junction
- D. go around the cyclist on the junction

342

A horse rider is in the left-hand lane approaching a roundabout. You should expect the rider to

Mark one answer
- A. go in any direction
- B. turn right
- C. turn left
- D. go ahead

343

You have just passed your test. How can you reduce your risk of being involved in a collision?

Mark one answer
- A. By always staying close to the vehicle in front
- B. By never going over 40mph
- C. By staying only in the left-hand lane on all roads
- D. By taking further training

344

Powered vehicles used by disabled people are small and hard to see. How do they give early warning when on a dual carriageway?

Mark one answer

- [ ] A. They will have a flashing red light
- [ ] B. They will have a flashing green light
- [ ] C. They will have a flashing blue light
- [ ] D. They will have a flashing amber light

345

You should never attempt to overtake a cyclist

Mark one answer

- [ ] A. just before you turn left
- [ ] B. on a left-hand bend
- [ ] C. on a one-way street
- [ ] D. on a dual carriageway

346

Ahead of you there is a moving vehicle with a flashing amber beacon. This means it is

Mark one answer

- [ ] A. slow moving
- [ ] B. broken down
- [ ] C. a doctor's car
- [ ] D. a school crossing patrol

347

Some junctions controlled by traffic lights have a marked area between two stop lines. What is this for?

Mark one answer

- [ ] A. To allow taxis to position in front of other traffic
- [ ] B. To allow people with disabilities to cross the road
- [ ] C. To allow cyclists and pedestrians to cross the road together
- [ ] D. To allow cyclists to position in front of other traffic

348

At some traffic lights there are advance stop lines and a marked area. What are these for?

Mark one answer

- [ ] A. To allow cyclists to position in front of other traffic
- [ ] B. To let pedestrians cross when the lights change
- [ ] C. To prevent traffic from jumping the lights
- [ ] D. To let passengers get off a bus which is queuing

349 You are riding behind a long vehicle. There is a mini-roundabout ahead. The vehicle is signalling left, but positioned to the right. You should

Mark one answer

- A. sound your horn
- B. overtake on the left
- C. keep well back
- D. flash your headlights

350 Why should you be careful when riding on roads where electric trams operate?

Mark two answers

- A. They cannot steer to avoid you
- B. They move quickly and quietly
- C. They are noisy and slow
- D. They can steer to avoid you
- E. They give off harmful exhaust fumes

351 You are about to overtake a slow-moving motorcyclist. Which one of these signs would make you take special care?

Mark one answer

A.

B.

C.

D.

352 You are waiting to emerge left from a minor road. A large vehicle is approaching from the right. You have time to turn, but you should wait. Why?

Mark one answer

- A. The large vehicle can easily hide an overtaking vehicle
- B. The large vehicle can turn suddenly
- C. The large vehicle is difficult to steer in a straight line
- D. The large vehicle can easily hide vehicles from the left

353 You are following a long vehicle. It approaches a crossroads and signals left, but moves out to the right. You should

Mark one answer

- A. get closer in order to pass it quickly
- B. stay well back and give it room
- C. assume the signal is wrong and it is really turning right
- D. overtake as it starts to slow down

354

You are following a long vehicle approaching a crossroads. The driver signals right but moves close to the left-hand kerb. What should you do?

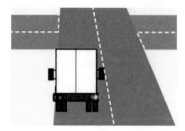

Mark one answer

- [ ] **A.** Warn the driver of the wrong signal
- [ ] **B.** Wait behind the long vehicle
- [ ] **C.** Report the driver to the police
- [ ] **D.** Overtake on the right-hand side

355

You are approaching a mini-roundabout. The long vehicle in front is signalling left but positioned over to the right. You should

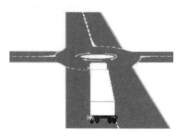

Mark one answer

- [ ] **A.** sound your horn
- [ ] **B.** overtake on the left
- [ ] **C.** follow the same course as the lorry
- [ ] **D.** keep well back

356

Before overtaking a large vehicle you should keep well back. Why is this?

Mark one answer

- [ ] **A.** To give acceleration space to overtake quickly on blind bends
- [ ] **B.** To get the best view of the road ahead
- [ ] **C.** To leave a gap in case the vehicle stops and rolls back
- [ ] **D.** To offer other drivers a safe gap if they want to overtake you

357

Why is it more difficult to overtake a large vehicle than a car?

Mark one answer

- [ ] **A.** It takes longer to pass one
- [ ] **B.** They may suddenly pull up
- [ ] **C.** Their brakes are not as good
- [ ] **D.** They climb hills more slowly

358

You are travelling behind a bus that pulls up at a bus stop. What should you do?

Mark two answers

- [ ] **A.** Accelerate past the bus sounding your horn
- [ ] **B.** Watch carefully for pedestrians
- [ ] **C.** Be ready to give way to the bus
- [ ] **D.** Pull in closely behind the bus

359 When you approach a bus signalling to move off from a bus stop you should

Mark one answer
- [ ] **A.** get past before it moves
- [ ] **B.** allow it to pull away, if it is safe to do so
- [ ] **C.** flash your headlights as you approach
- [ ] **D.** signal left and wave the bus on

360 Which of these is LEAST likely to be affected by crosswinds?

Mark one answer
- [ ] **A.** Cyclists
- [ ] **B.** Motorcyclists
- [ ] **C.** High-sided vehicles
- [ ] **D.** Cars

361 You are following a large lorry on a wet road. Spray makes it difficult to see. You should

Mark one answer
- [ ] **A.** drop back until you can see better
- [ ] **B.** put your headlights on full beam
- [ ] **C.** keep close to the lorry, away from the spray
- [ ] **D.** speed up and overtake quickly

362 What should you do as you approach this lorry?

Mark one answer
- [ ] **A.** Slow down and be prepared to wait
- [ ] **B.** Make the lorry wait for you
- [ ] **C.** Flash your lights at the lorry
- [ ] **D.** Move to the right-hand side of the road

363 You are following a large articulated vehicle. It is going to turn left into a narrow road. What action should you take?

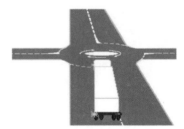

Mark one answer
- [ ] **A.** Move out and overtake on the right
- [ ] **B.** Pass on the left as the vehicle moves out
- [ ] **C.** Be prepared to stop behind
- [ ] **D.** Overtake quickly before the lorry moves out

364 You keep well back while waiting to overtake a large vehicle. A car fills the gap. You should

Mark one answer

- [ ] **A.** sound your horn
- [ ] **B.** drop back further
- [ ] **C.** flash your headlights
- [ ] **D.** start to overtake

365 You are following a large vehicle approaching crossroads. The driver signals to turn left. What should you do?

Mark one answer

- [ ] **A.** Overtake if you can leave plenty of room
- [ ] **B.** Overtake only if there are no oncoming vehicles
- [ ] **C.** Do not overtake until the vehicle begins to turn
- [ ] **D.** Do not overtake when at or approaching a junction

366 You are following a long lorry. The driver signals to turn left into a narrow road. What should you do?

Mark one answer

- [ ] **A.** Overtake on the left before the lorry reaches the junction
- [ ] **B.** Overtake on the right as soon as the lorry slows down
- [ ] **C.** Do not overtake unless you can see there is no oncoming traffic
- [ ] **D.** Do not overtake, stay well back and be prepared to stop

367 You wish to overtake a long, slow-moving vehicle on a busy road. You should

Mark one answer

- [ ] **A.** follow it closely and keep moving out to see the road ahead
- [ ] **B.** flash your headlights for the oncoming traffic to give way
- [ ] **C.** stay behind until the driver waves you past
- [ ] **D.** keep well back until you can see that it is clear

368 Powered vehicles, such as wheelchairs or scooters, used by disabled people have a maximum speed of

Mark one answer

- [ ] **A.** 8mph
- [ ] **B.** 12mph
- [ ] **C.** 16mph
- [ ] **D.** 20mph

369 In front of you is a class 3 powered vehicle (powered wheelchair) driven by a disabled person. These vehicles have a maximum speed of

Mark one answer

- [ ] **A.** 8mph (12km/h)
- [ ] **B.** 18mph (29km/h)
- [ ] **C.** 28mph (45km/h)
- [ ] **D.** 38mph (61km/h)

370 You are sitting on a stationary motorcycle and checking your riding position. You should be able to

Mark one answer
- [ ] **A.** just touch the ground with your toes
- [ ] **B.** place both feet on the ground
- [ ] **C.** operate the centre stand
- [ ] **D.** adjust your mirrors by stretching

371 As a safety measure before starting your engine, you should

Mark two answers
- [ ] **A.** push the motorcycle forward to check the rear wheel turns freely
- [ ] **B.** engage first gear and apply the rear brake
- [ ] **C.** engage first gear and apply the front brake
- [ ] **D.** glance at the neutral light on your instrument panel

372 Your motorcycle does NOT have linked brakes. What should you do when braking to a normal stop?

Mark one answer
- [ ] **A.** only apply the front brake
- [ ] **B.** rely just on the rear brake
- [ ] **C.** apply both brakes smoothly
- [ ] **D.** apply either of the brakes gently

373 You are going ahead and will have to cross tram lines. Why should you be especially careful?

Mark one answer
- [ ] **A.** Tram lines are always 'live'
- [ ] **B.** Trams will be stopping here
- [ ] **C.** Pedestrians will be crossing here
- [ ] **D.** The steel rails can be slippery

374 You are approaching this junction. As the motorcyclist you should

Mark two answers
- [ ] **A.** prepare to slow down
- [ ] **B.** sound your horn
- [ ] **C.** keep near the left kerb
- [ ] **D.** speed up to clear the junction
- [ ] **E.** stop, as the car has right of way

375 What can you do to improve your safety on the road as a motorcyclist?

Mark one answer
- [ ] **A.** Anticipate the actions of others
- [ ] **B.** Stay just above the speed limits
- [ ] **C.** Keep positioned close to the kerbs
- [ ] **D.** Remain well below speed limits

376 Which THREE of these can cause skidding?

Mark three answers
- [ ] **A.** Braking too gently
- [ ] **B.** Leaning too far over when cornering
- [ ] **C.** Staying upright when cornering
- [ ] **D.** Braking too hard
- [ ] **E.** Changing direction suddenly

377 It is very cold and the road looks wet. You cannot hear any road noise. You should

Mark two answers

- [ ] A. continue riding at the same speed
- [ ] B. ride slower in as high a gear as possible
- [ ] C. ride in as low a gear as possible
- [ ] D. keep revving your engine
- [ ] E. slow down as there may be black ice

378 When riding a motorcycle you should wear full protective clothing

Mark one answer

- [ ] A. at all times
- [ ] B. only on faster, open roads
- [ ] C. just on long journeys
- [ ] D. only during bad weather

379 You have to make a journey in fog. What are the TWO most important things you should do before you set out?

Mark two answers

- [ ] A. Fill up with fuel
- [ ] B. Make sure that you have a warm drink with you
- [ ] C. Check that your lights are working
- [ ] D. Check the battery
- [ ] E. Make sure that your visor is clean

380 The best place to park your motorcycle is

Mark one answer

- [ ] A. on soft tarmac
- [ ] B. on bumpy ground
- [ ] C. on grass
- [ ] D. on firm, level ground

381 When riding in windy conditions, you should

Mark one answer

- [ ] A. stay close to large vehicles
- [ ] B. keep your speed up
- [ ] C. keep your speed down
- [ ] D. stay close to the gutter

382 In normal riding your position on the road should be

Mark one answer

- [ ] A. about a foot from the kerb
- [ ] B. about central in your lane
- [ ] C. on the right of your lane
- [ ] D. near the centre of the road

383 Your motorcycle is parked on a two-way road. You should get on from the

Mark one answer

- [ ] A. right and apply the rear brake
- [ ] B. left and leave the brakes alone
- [ ] C. left and apply the front brake
- [ ] D. right and leave the brakes alone

384 To gain basic skills in how to ride a motorcycle you should

Mark one answer

- [ ] A. practise off-road with an approved training body
- [ ] B. ride on the road on the first dry day
- [ ] C. practise off-road in a public park or in a quiet cul-de-sac
- [ ] D. ride on the road as soon as possible

385
You should not ride with your clutch lever pulled in for longer than necessary because it

Mark one answer
- [ ] **A.** increases wear on the gearbox
- [ ] **B.** increases petrol consumption
- [ ] **C.** reduces your control of the motorcycle
- [ ] **D.** reduces the grip of the tyres

386
You are approaching a road with a surface of loose chippings. What should you do?

Mark one answer
- [ ] **A.** Ride normally
- [ ] **B.** Speed up
- [ ] **C.** Slow down
- [ ] **D.** Stop suddenly

387
It rains after a long dry, hot spell. This may cause the road surface to

Mark one answer
- [ ] **A.** be unusually slippery
- [ ] **B.** give better grip
- [ ] **C.** become covered in grit
- [ ] **D.** melt and break up

388
The main causes of a motorcycle skidding are

Mark three answers
- [ ] **A.** heavy and sharp braking
- [ ] **B.** excessive acceleration
- [ ] **C.** leaning too far when cornering
- [ ] **D.** riding in wet weather
- [ ] **E.** riding in the winter

389
To stop your motorcycle quickly in an emergency you should apply

Mark one answer
- [ ] **A.** the rear brake only
- [ ] **B.** the front brake only
- [ ] **C.** the front brake just before the rear
- [ ] **D.** the rear brake just before the front

390
Riding with the side stand down could cause you to crash. This is most likely to happen when

Mark one answer
- [ ] **A.** going uphill
- [ ] **B.** accelerating
- [ ] **C.** braking
- [ ] **D.** cornering

391
You leave the choke on for too long. This causes the engine to run too fast. When is this likely to make your motorcycle most difficult to control?

Mark one answer
- [ ] **A.** Accelerating
- [ ] **B.** Going uphill
- [ ] **C.** Slowing down
- [ ] **D.** On motorways

392
You should NOT look down at the front wheel when riding because it can

Mark one answer
- [ ] **A.** make your steering lighter
- [ ] **B.** improve your balance
- [ ] **C.** use less fuel
- [ ] **D.** upset your balance

393
You are entering a bend. Your side stand is not fully raised. This could

Mark one answer
- [ ] **A.** cause you to crash
- [ ] **B.** improve your balance
- [ ] **C.** alter the motorcycle's centre of gravity
- [ ] **D.** make the motorcycle more stable

394
In normal riding conditions you should brake

Mark one answer
- [ ] **A.** by using the rear brake first and then the front
- [ ] **B.** when the motorcycle is being turned or ridden through a bend
- [ ] **C.** by pulling in the clutch before using the front brake
- [ ] **D.** when the motorcycle is upright and moving in a straight line

395
You have to brake sharply and your motorcycle starts to skid. You should

Mark one answer
- [ ] **A.** continue braking and select a low gear
- [ ] **B.** apply the brakes harder for better grip
- [ ] **C.** select neutral and use the front brake only
- [ ] **D.** release the brakes and reapply

396
Which THREE of the following will affect your stopping distance?

Mark three answers
- [ ] **A.** How fast you are going
- [ ] **B.** The tyres on your motorcycle
- [ ] **C.** The time of day
- [ ] **D.** The weather
- [ ] **E.** The street lighting

397
You are on a motorway at night. You MUST have your headlights switched on unless

Mark one answer
- [ ] **A.** there are vehicles close in front of you
- [ ] **B.** you are travelling below 50mph
- [ ] **C.** the motorway is lit
- [ ] **D.** your motorcycle is broken down on the hard shoulder

398
You have to park on the road in fog. You should

Mark one answer
- [ ] **A.** leave parking lights on
- [ ] **B.** leave no lights on
- [ ] **C.** leave dipped headlights on
- [ ] **D.** leave main beam headlights on

399
You ride over broken glass and get a sudden puncture. What should you do?

Mark one answer
- [ ] **A.** Close the throttle and roll to a stop
- [ ] **B.** Brake to a stop as quickly as possible
- [ ] **C.** Release your grip on the handlebars
- [ ] **D.** Steer from side to side to keep your balance

400
You see a rainbow-coloured pattern across the road. What will this warn you of?

Mark one answer
- A. A soft uneven road surface
- B. A polished road surface
- C. Fuel spilt on the road
- D. Water on the road

401
You are riding in wet weather. You see diesel fuel on the road. What should you do?

Mark one answer
- A. Swerve to avoid the area
- B. Accelerate through quickly
- C. Brake sharply to a stop
- D. Slow down in good time

402
Spilt fuel on the road can be very dangerous for you as a motorcyclist. How can this hazard be seen?

Mark one answer
- A. By a rainbow pattern on the surface
- B. By a series of skid marks
- C. By a pitted road surface
- D. By a highly polished surface

403
Traction Control Systems (TCS) are fitted to some motorcycles. What does this help to prevent?

Mark one answer
- A. Wheelspin when accelerating
- B. Skidding when braking too hard
- C. Uneven front tyre wear
- D. Uneven rear tyre wear

404
Braking too hard has caused both wheels to skid. What should you do?

Mark one answer
- A. Release both brakes together
- B. Release the front then the rear brake
- C. Release the front brake only
- D. Release the rear brake only

405
You leave the choke on for too long. This could make the engine run faster than normal. This will make your motorcycle

Mark one answer
- A. handle much better
- B. corner much safer
- C. stop much more quickly
- D. more difficult to control

406
Which FOUR types of road surface increase the risk of skidding for motorcyclists?

Mark four answers
- A. White lines
- B. Dry tarmac
- C. Tar banding
- D. Yellow grid lines
- E. Loose chippings

407 You are riding on a wet road. When braking you should

Mark one answer

- A. apply the rear brake well before the front
- B. apply the front brake just before the rear
- C. avoid using the front brake at all
- D. avoid using the rear brake at all

408 The road is wet. You are passing a line of queuing traffic and riding on the painted road markings. You should take extra care, particularly when

Mark one answer

- A. signalling
- B. braking
- C. carrying a passenger
- D. checking your mirrors

409 In which THREE of these situations may you overtake another vehicle on the left?

Mark three answers

- A. When you are in a one-way street
- B. When approaching a motorway slip road where you will be turning off
- C. When the vehicle in front is signalling to turn right
- D. When a slower vehicle is travelling in the right-hand lane of a dual carriageway
- E. In slow-moving traffic queues when traffic in the right-hand lane is moving more slowly

410 You are travelling in very heavy rain. Your overall stopping distance is likely to be

Mark one answer

- A. doubled
- B. halved
- C. up to ten times greater
- D. no different

411 Which TWO of the following are correct? When overtaking at night you should

Mark two answers

- A. wait until a bend so that you can see the oncoming headlights
- B. sound your horn twice before moving out
- C. be careful because you can see less
- D. beware of bends in the road ahead
- E. put headlights on full beam

412 When may you wait in a box junction?

Mark one answer

- A. When you are stationary in a queue of traffic
- B. When approaching a pelican crossing
- C. When approaching a zebra crossing
- D. When oncoming traffic prevents you turning right

413 Which of these plates normally appear with this road sign?

Mark one answer

☐ A. **Humps for ½ mile**

☐ B. **Hump Bridge**

☐ C. **Low Bridge**

☐ D. **Soft Verge**

414 Areas reserved for trams may have

Mark three answers

☐ A. metal studs around them
☐ B. white line markings
☐ C. zigzag markings
☐ D. a different coloured surface
☐ E. yellow hatch markings
☐ F. a different surface texture

415 Traffic calming measures are used to

Mark one answer

☐ A. stop road rage
☐ B. help overtaking
☐ C. slow traffic down
☐ D. help parking

416 Why should you always reduce your speed when travelling in fog?

Mark one answer

☐ A. The brakes do not work as well
☐ B. You will be dazzled by other headlights
☐ C. The engine will take longer to warm up
☐ D. It is more difficult to see events ahead

417 You are on a motorway in fog. The left-hand edge of the motorway can be identified by reflective studs. What colour are they?

Mark one answer

☐ A. Green   ☐ B. Amber
☐ C. Red   ☐ D. White

418 A rumble device is designed to

Mark two answers

☐ A. give directions
☐ B. prevent cattle escaping
☐ C. alert you to low tyre pressure
☐ D. alert you to a hazard
☐ E. encourage you to reduce speed

419 After this hazard you should test your brakes. Why is this?

Ford

Mark one answer

- **A.** You will be on a slippery road
- **B.** Your brakes will be soaking wet
- **C.** You will have going down a long hill
- **D.** You will have just crossed a long bridge

420 You have to make a journey in foggy conditions. You should

Mark one answer

- **A.** follow other vehicles' tail-lights closely
- **B.** avoid using dipped headlights
- **C.** leave plenty of time for your journey
- **D.** keep two seconds behind other vehicles

421 You see a vehicle coming towards you on a single-track road. You should

Mark one answer

- **A.** go back to the main road
- **B.** do an emergency stop
- **C.** stop at a passing place
- **D.** put on your hazard warning lights

422 You are overtaking a car at night. You must be sure that

Mark one answer

- **A.** you flash your headlights before overtaking
- **B.** you select a higher gear
- **C.** you have switched your lights to full beam before overtaking
- **D.** you do not dazzle other road users

423 You are on a road which has speed humps. A driver in front is travelling slower than you. You should

Mark one answer
- [ ] **A.** sound your horn
- [ ] **B.** overtake as soon as you can
- [ ] **C.** flash your headlights
- [ ] **D.** slow down and stay behind

424 You see these markings on the road. Why are they there?

Mark one answer
- [ ] **A.** To show a safe distance between vehicles
- [ ] **B.** To keep the area clear of traffic
- [ ] **C.** To make you aware of your speed
- [ ] **D.** To warn you to change direction

425 The road is wet. Why might a motorcyclist steer round drain covers on a bend?

Mark one answer
- [ ] **A.** To avoid puncturing the tyres on the edge of the drain covers
- [ ] **B.** To prevent the motorcycle sliding on the metal drain covers
- [ ] **C.** To help judge the bend using the drain covers as marker points
- [ ] **D.** To avoid splashing pedestrians on the pavement

426 It has rained after a long dry spell. You should be very careful because the road surface will be unusually

Mark one answer
- [ ] **A.** rough
- [ ] **B.** dry
- [ ] **C.** sticky
- [ ] **D.** slippery

427 A motorcycle is not allowed on a motorway if it has an engine size smaller than

Mark one answer

- [ ] **A.** 50cc
- [ ] **C.** 150cc
- [ ] **B.** 125cc
- [ ] **D.** 250cc

428 You are riding on a motorway. Unless signs show otherwise you must NOT exceed

Mark one answer   **NI**

- [ ] **A.** 50mph
- [ ] **B.** 60mph
- [ ] **C.** 70mph
- [ ] **D.** 80mph

429 To ride on a motorway your motorcycle must be

Mark one answer

- [ ] **A.** 50cc or more
- [ ] **B.** 100cc or more
- [ ] **C.** 125cc or more
- [ ] **D.** 250cc or more

430 On a three-lane motorway why should you normally ride in the left-hand lane?

Mark one answer

- [ ] **A.** The left-hand lane is only for lorries and motorcycles
- [ ] **B.** The left-hand lane should only be used by smaller vehicles
- [ ] **C.** The lanes on the right are for overtaking
- [ ] **D.** Motorcycles are not allowed in the far right-hand lane

431 You are riding at 70mph on a three-lane motorway. There is no traffic ahead. Which lane should you use?

Mark one answer

- [ ] **A.** Any lane
- [ ] **C.** Right-hand lane
- [ ] **B.** Middle lane
- [ ] **D.** Left-hand lane

432 Why is it particularly important to carry out a check of your motorcycle before making a long motorway journey?

Mark one answer

- [ ] **A.** You will have to do more harsh braking on motorways
- [ ] **B.** Motorway service stations do not deal with breakdowns
- [ ] **C.** The road surface will wear down the tyres faster
- [ ] **D.** Continuous high speeds may increase the risk of your motorcycle breaking down

433 On a motorway you may ONLY stop on the hard shoulder

Mark one answer

- [ ] **A.** in an emergency
- [ ] **B.** if you feel tired and need to rest
- [ ] **C.** if you go past the exit that you wanted to take
- [ ] **D.** to pick up a hitchhiker

434 You are intending to leave the motorway at the next exit. Before you reach the exit you should normally position your motorcycle

Mark one answer

- A. in the middle lane
- B. in the left-hand lane
- C. on the hard shoulder
- D. in any lane

435 You are joining a motorway from a slip road. You should

Mark one answer

- A. adjust your speed to the speed of the traffic on the motorway
- B. accelerate as quickly as you can and ride straight out
- C. ride on to the hard shoulder until a gap appears
- D. expect drivers on the motorway to give way to you

436 Which FOUR of these must NOT use motorways?

Mark four answers

- A. Learner car drivers
- B. Motorcycles over 50cc
- C. Double-deck buses
- D. Farm tractors
- E. Horse riders
- F. Cyclists

437 Which FOUR of these must NOT use motorways?

Mark four answers

- A. Learner car drivers
- B. Motorcycles over 50cc
- C. Double-deck buses
- D. Farm tractors
- E. Learner motorcyclists
- F. Cyclists

438 Immediately after joining a motorway you should normally

Mark one answer

- A. try to overtake
- B. re-adjust your mirrors
- C. position your vehicle in the centre lane
- D. keep in the left-hand lane

439 When joining a motorway you must always

Mark one answer

- A. use the hard shoulder
- B. stop at the end of the acceleration lane
- C. come to a stop before joining the motorway
- D. give way to traffic already on the motorway

440 What is the national speed limit for cars and motorcycles in the centre lane of a three-lane motorway?

Mark one answer

- A. 40mph
- B. 50mph
- C. 60mph
- D. 70mph

441 What is the national speed limit on motorways for cars and motorcycles?

Mark one answer

- [ ] A. 30mph
- [ ] B. 50mph
- [ ] C. 60mph
- [ ] D. 70mph

442 The left-hand lane on a three-lane motorway is for use by

Mark one answer

- [ ] A. any vehicle
- [ ] B. large vehicles only
- [ ] C. emergency vehicles only
- [ ] D. slow vehicles only

443 What is the right-hand lane used for on a three-lane motorway?

Mark one answer

- [ ] A. Emergency vehicles only
- [ ] B. Overtaking
- [ ] C. Vehicles towing trailers
- [ ] D. Coaches only

444 Which of these IS NOT allowed to travel in the right-hand lane of a three-lane motorway?

Mark one answer

- [ ] A. A small delivery van
- [ ] B. A motorcycle
- [ ] C. A vehicle towing a trailer
- [ ] D. A motorcycle and sidecar

445 You are travelling on a motorway. You decide you need a rest. You should

Mark one answer

- [ ] A. stop on the hard shoulder
- [ ] B. pull in at the nearest service station
- [ ] C. pull up on a slip road
- [ ] D. park on the central reservation

446 You break down on a motorway. You need to call for help. Why may it be better to use an emergency roadside telephone rather than a mobile phone?

Mark one answer

- [ ] A. It connects you to a local garage
- [ ] B. Using a mobile phone will distract other drivers
- [ ] C. It allows easy location by the emergency services
- [ ] D. Mobile phones do not work on motorways

447 What should you use the hard shoulder of a motorway for?

Mark one answer

- [ ] A. Stopping in an emergency
- [ ] B. Leaving the motorway
- [ ] C. Stopping when you are tired
- [ ] D. Joining the motorway

448 After a breakdown you need to rejoin the main carriageway of a motorway from the hard shoulder. You should

Mark one answer

- [ ] **A.** move out onto the carriageway then build up your speed
- [ ] **B.** move out onto the carriageway using your hazard lights
- [ ] **C.** gain speed on the hard shoulder before moving out onto the carriageway
- [ ] **D.** wait on the hard shoulder until someone flashes their headlights at you

449 A crawler lane on a motorway is found

Mark one answer

- [ ] **A.** on a steep gradient
- [ ] **B.** before a service area
- [ ] **C.** before a junction
- [ ] **D.** along the hard shoulder

450 You are on a motorway. There are red flashing lights above every lane. You must

Mark one answer

- [ ] **A.** pull on to the hard shoulder
- [ ] **B.** slow down and watch for further signals
- [ ] **C.** leave at the next exit
- [ ] **D.** stop and wait

451 You are in the right-hand lane on a motorway. You see these overhead signs. This means

Mark one answer

- [ ] **A.** move to the left and reduce your speed to 50mph
- [ ] **B.** there are roadworks 50 metres (55 yards) ahead
- [ ] **C.** use the hard shoulder until you have passed the hazard
- [ ] **D.** leave the motorway at the next exit

452 What do these motorway signs show?

Mark one answer

- [ ] **A.** They are countdown markers to a bridge
- [ ] **B.** They are distance markers to the next telephone
- [ ] **C.** They are countdown markers to the next exit
- [ ] **D.** They warn of a police control ahead

453 On a motorway the amber reflective studs can be found between

Mark one answer

- A. the hard shoulder and the carriageway
- B. the acceleration lane and the carriageway
- C. the central reservation and the carriageway
- D. each pair of the lanes

454 What colour are the reflective studs between the lanes on a motorway?

Mark one answer

- A. Green
- B. Amber
- C. White
- D. Red

455 What colour are the reflective studs between a motorway and its slip road?

Mark one answer

- A. Amber
- B. White
- C. Green
- D. Red

456 You are allowed to stop on a motorway when you

Mark one answer

- A. need to walk and get fresh air
- B. wish to pick up hitchhikers
- C. are told to do so by flashing red lights
- D. need to use a mobile telephone

457 You have broken down on a motorway. To find the nearest emergency telephone you should always walk

Mark one answer

- A. with the traffic flow
- B. facing oncoming traffic
- C. in the direction shown on the marker posts
- D. in the direction of the nearest exit

458 You are travelling along the left-hand lane of a three-lane motorway. Traffic is joining from a slip road. You should

Mark one answer

- A. race the other vehicles
- B. move to another lane
- C. maintain a steady speed
- D. switch on your hazard flashers

459 You are joining a motorway. Why is it important to make full use of the slip road?

Mark one answer

- A. Because there is space available to turn round if you need to
- B. To allow you direct access to the overtaking lanes
- C. To build up a speed similar to traffic on the motorway
- D. Because you can continue on the hard shoulder

460 How should you use the emergency telephone on a motorway?

Mark one answer

- A. Stay close to the carriageway
- B. Face the oncoming traffic
- C. Keep your back to the traffic
- D. Stand on the hard shoulder

461
You are on a motorway. What colour are the reflective studs on the left of the carriageway?

Mark one answer

- A. Green
- B. Red
- C. White
- D. Amber

462
On a three-lane motorway which lane should you normally use?

Mark one answer

- A. Left
- B. Right
- C. Centre
- D. Either the right or centre

463
A basic rule when on motorways is

Mark one answer

- A. use the lane that has least traffic
- B. keep to the left-hand lane unless overtaking
- C. overtake on the side that is clearest
- D. try to keep above 50mph to prevent congestion

464
When going through a contraflow system on a motorway you should

Mark one answer

- A. ensure that you do not exceed 30mph
- B. keep a good distance from the vehicle ahead
- C. switch lanes to keep the traffic flowing
- D. stay close to the vehicle ahead to reduce queues

465
You are on a three-lane motorway. There are red reflective studs on your left and white ones to your right. Where are you?

Mark one answer

- A. In the right-hand lane
- B. In the middle lane
- C. On the hard shoulder
- D. In the left-hand lane

466
When should you stop on a motorway?

Mark three answers

- A. If you have to read a map
- B. When you are tired and need a rest
- C. If red lights show above every lane
- D. When told to by the police
- E. If your mobile phone rings
- F. When signalled by a Highways Agency Traffic Officer

467
You are approaching roadworks on a motorway. What should you do?

Mark one answer

- A. Speed up to clear the area quickly
- B. Always use the hard shoulder
- C. Obey all speed limits
- D. Stay very close to the vehicle in front

468 On motorways you should never overtake on the left unless

Mark one answer

- [ ] A. you can see well ahead that the hard shoulder is clear
- [ ] B. the traffic in the right-hand lane is signalling right
- [ ] C. you warn drivers behind by signalling left
- [ ] D. there is a queue of slow-moving traffic to your right that is moving more slowly than you are

469 You are travelling on a motorway. Unless signs show a lower speed limit you must NOT exceed

NI

Mark one answer

- [ ] A. 50mph
- [ ] B. 60mph
- [ ] C. 70mph
- [ ] D. 80mph

470 For what reason may you use the right-hand lane of a motorway?

Mark one answer

- [ ] A. For keeping out of the way of lorries
- [ ] B. For travelling at more than 70mph
- [ ] C. For turning right
- [ ] D. For overtaking other vehicles

471 Motorway emergency telephones are usually linked to the police. In some areas they are now linked to

Mark one answer

- [ ] A. the local ambulance service
- [ ] B. an Highways Agency control centre
- [ ] C. the local fire brigade
- [ ] D. a breakdown service control centre

472 Motorway emergency telephones are usually linked to the police. In some areas they are now linked to

Mark one answer **NI**

- [ ] A. the Highways Agency Control Centre
- [ ] B. the Driver Vehicle Licensing Agency
- [ ] C. the Driving Standards Agency
- [ ] D. the local Vehicle Registration Office

473 An Emergency Refuge Area is an area

Mark one answer

- [ ] A. on a motorway for use in cases of emergency or breakdown
- [ ] B. for use if you think you will be involved in a road rage incident
- [ ] C. on a motorway for a police patrol to park and watch traffic
- [ ] D. for construction and road workers to store emergency equipment

474 What is an Emergency Refuge Area on a motorway for?

Mark one answer

- [ ] A. An area to park in when you want to use a mobile phone
- [ ] B. To use in cases of emergency or breakdown
- [ ] C. For an emergency recovery vehicle to park in a contraflow system
- [ ] D. To drive in when there is queuing traffic ahead

475 Highways Agency Traffic Officers

Mark one answer **NI**

- A. will not be able to assist at a breakdown or emergency
- B. are not able to stop and direct anyone on a motorway
- C. will tow a broken down vehicle and its passengers home
- D. are able to stop and direct anyone on a motorway

476 You are on a motorway. A red cross is displayed above the hard shoulder. What does this mean?

Mark one answer **NI**

- A. Pull up in this lane to answer your mobile phone
- B. Use this lane as a running lane
- C. This lane can be used if you need a rest
- D. You should not travel in this lane

477 You are on a motorway in an Active Traffic Management (ATM) area. A mandatory speed limit is displayed above the hard shoulder. What does this mean?

Mark one answer **NI**

- A. You should not travel in this lane
- B. The hard shoulder can be used as a running lane
- C. You can park on the hard shoulder if you feel tired
- D. You can pull up in this lane to answer a mobile phone

478 The aim of an Active Traffic Management scheme on a motorway is to

Mark one answer **NI**

- A. prevent overtaking
- B. reduce rest stops
- C. prevent tailgating
- D. reduce congestion

479 You are in an Active Traffic Management area on a motorway. When the Actively Managed mode is operating

Mark one answer **NI**

- A. speed limits are only advisory
- B. the national speed limit will apply
- C. the speed limit is always 30mph
- D. all speed limit signals are set

480 You are on a three-lane motorway. A red cross is shown above the hard shoulder and mandatory speed limits above all other lanes. This means

Mark one answer **NI**

- A. the hard shoulder can be used as a rest area if you feel tired
- B. the hard shoulder is for emergency or breakdown use only
- C. the hard shoulder can be used as a normal running lane
- D. the hard shoulder has a speed limit of 50mph

481 You are travelling on a motorway. A red cross is shown above the hard shoulder. What does this mean?

Mark one answer **NI**

- A. Use this lane as a rest area
- B. Use this as a normal running lane
- C. Do not use this lane to travel in
- D. National speed limit applies in this lane

482 You are on a three-lane motorway and see this sign. It means you can use

Mark one answer **NI**

- A. any lane except the hard shoulder
- B. the hard shoulder only
- C. the three right hand lanes only
- D. all the lanes including the hard shoulder

483
Why can it be an advantage for traffic speed to stay constant over a longer distance?

Mark one answer

- A. You will do more stop-start driving
- B. You will use far more fuel
- C. You will be able to use more direct routes
- D. Your overall journey time will normally improve

484
You should not normally travel on the hard shoulder of a motorway. When can you use it?

Mark one answer   **NI**

- A. When taking the next exit
- B. When traffic is stopped
- C. When signs direct you to
- D. When traffic is slow moving

485
On a motorway what is used to reduce traffic bunching?

Mark one answer

- A. Variable speed limits
- B. Contraflow systems
- C. National speed limits
- D. Lane closures

486
When may you stop on a motorway?

Mark one answer

- A. If you have to read a map
- B. When you are tired and need a rest
- C. If your mobile phone rings
- D. In an emergency or breakdown

487
You are on a motorway. You become tired and decide you need to rest. What should you do?

Mark one answer

- A. Stop on the hard shoulder
- B. Pull up on a slip road
- C. Park on the central reservation
- D. Leave at the next exit

488
You are riding slowly in a town centre. Before turning left you should glance over your left shoulder to

Mark one answer
- [ ] **A.** check for cyclists
- [ ] **B.** help keep your balance
- [ ] **C.** look for traffic signs
- [ ] **D.** check for potholes

489
As a motorcycle rider which TWO lanes must you NOT use?

Mark two answers
- [ ] **A.** Crawler lane
- [ ] **B.** Overtaking lane
- [ ] **C.** Acceleration lane
- [ ] **D.** Cycle lane
- [ ] **E.** Tram lane

490
When filtering through slow-moving or stationary traffic you should

Mark three answers
- [ ] **A.** watch for hidden vehicles emerging from side roads
- [ ] **B.** continually use your horn as a warning
- [ ] **C.** look for vehicles changing course suddenly
- [ ] **D.** always ride with your hazard lights on
- [ ] **E.** stand up on the footrests for a good view ahead
- [ ] **F.** look for pedestrians walking between vehicles

491
You want to tow a trailer with your motorcycle. Your engine must be more than

Mark one answer
- [ ] **A.** 50cc
- [ ] **B.** 125cc
- [ ] **C.** 525cc
- [ ] **D.** 1,000cc

492
What is the national speed limit on a single carriageway?

Mark one answer
- [ ] **A.** 40mph
- [ ] **B.** 50mph
- [ ] **C.** 60mph
- [ ] **D.** 70mph

493
What does this sign mean?

Mark one answer
- [ ] **A.** No parking for solo motorcycles
- [ ] **B.** Parking for solo motorcycles
- [ ] **C.** Passing place for motorcycles
- [ ] **D.** Police motorcycles only

494
You are riding towards roadworks. The temporary traffic lights are at red. The road ahead is clear. What should you do?

Mark one answer
- [ ] **A.** Ride on with extreme caution
- [ ] **B.** Ride on at normal speed
- [ ] **C.** Carry on if approaching cars have stopped
- [ ] **D.** Wait for the green light

495
You are riding on a busy dual carriageway. When changing lanes you should

Mark one answer
- [ ] **A.** rely totally on mirrors
- [ ] **B.** always increase your speed
- [ ] **C.** signal so others will give way
- [ ] **D.** use mirrors and shoulder checks

496
You are looking for somewhere to park your motorcycle. The area is full EXCEPT for spaces marked 'disabled use'. You can

Mark one answer
- [ ] A. use these spaces when elsewhere is full
- [ ] B. park if you stay with your motorcycle
- [ ] C. use these spaces, disabled or not
- [ ] D. not park there unless permitted

497
On which THREE occasions MUST you stop your motorcycle?

Mark three answers
- [ ] A. When involved in a collision
- [ ] B. At a red traffic light
- [ ] C. When signalled to do so by a police officer
- [ ] D. At a junction with double broken white lines
- [ ] E. At a clear pelican crossing when the amber light is flashing

498
You are on a road with passing places. It is only wide enough for one vehicle. There is a car coming towards you. What should you do?

Mark one answer
- [ ] A. Pull into a passing place on your right
- [ ] B. Force the other driver to reverse
- [ ] C. Turn round and ride back to the main road
- [ ] D. Pull into a passing place on your left

499
You intend to go abroad and will be riding on the right-hand side of the road. What should you fit to your motorcycle?

Mark one answer
- [ ] A. Twin headlights
- [ ] B. Headlight deflectors
- [ ] C. Tinted yellow brake lights
- [ ] D. Tinted red indicator lenses

500
You are both turning right at this crossroads. It is safer to keep the car to your right so you can

Mark one answer
- [ ] A. see approaching traffic
- [ ] B. keep close to the kerb
- [ ] C. keep clear of following traffic
- [ ] D. make oncoming vehicles stop

501
What is the meaning of this sign?

Mark one answer
- [ ] A. Local speed limit applies
- [ ] B. No waiting on the carriageway
- [ ] C. National speed limit applies
- [ ] D. No entry to vehicular traffic

502
What is the national speed limit on a single carriageway road for cars and motorcycles?

Mark one answer
- [ ] A. 30mph
- [ ] B. 50mph
- [ ] C. 60mph
- [ ] D. 70mph

503 What is the national speed limit for cars and motorcycles on a dual carriageway?

Mark one answer

- [ ] **A.** 30mph
- [ ] **B.** 50mph
- [ ] **C.** 60mph
- [ ] **D.** 70mph

504 There are no speed limit signs on the road. How is a 30mph limit indicated?

Mark one answer

- [ ] **A.** By hazard warning lines
- [ ] **B.** By street lighting
- [ ] **C.** By pedestrian islands
- [ ] **D.** By double or single yellow lines

505 Where you see street lights but no speed limit signs the limit is usually

Mark one answer

- [ ] **A.** 30mph
- [ ] **B.** 40mph
- [ ] **C.** 50mph
- [ ] **D.** 60mph

506 What does this sign mean?

Mark one answer

- [ ] **A.** Minimum speed 30mph
- [ ] **B.** End of maximum speed
- [ ] **C.** End of minimum speed
- [ ] **D.** Maximum speed 30mph

507 There is a tractor ahead of you. You wish to overtake but you are NOT sure if it is safe to do so. You should

Mark one answer

- [ ] **A.** follow another overtaking vehicle through
- [ ] **B.** sound your horn to the slow vehicle to pull over
- [ ] **C.** speed through but flash your lights to oncoming traffic
- [ ] **D.** not overtake if you are in doubt

508 Which three of the following are most likely to take an unusual course at roundabouts?

Mark three answers

- [ ] **A.** Horse riders
- [ ] **B.** Milk floats
- [ ] **C.** Delivery vans
- [ ] **D.** Long vehicles
- [ ] **E.** Estate cars
- [ ] **F.** Cyclists

509 In which TWO places should you NOT park?

Mark two answers

- [ ] **A.** Near a school entrance
- [ ] **B.** Near a police station
- [ ] **C.** In a side road
- [ ] **D.** At a bus stop
- [ ] **E.** In a one-way street

510 On a clearway you must not stop

Mark one answer

- [ ] **A.** at any time
- [ ] **B.** when it is busy
- [ ] **C.** in the rush hour
- [ ] **D.** during daylight hours

511 What is the meaning of this sign?

Mark one answer
- [ ] **A.** No entry
- [ ] **B.** Waiting restrictions
- [ ] **C.** National speed limit
- [ ] **D.** School crossing patrol

512 You can park on the right-hand side of a road at night

Mark one answer
- [ ] **A.** in a one-way street
- [ ] **B.** with your sidelights on
- [ ] **C.** more than 10 metres (32 feet) from a junction
- [ ] **D.** under a lamp-post

513 On a three-lane dual carriageway the right-hand lane can be used for

Mark one answer
- [ ] **A.** overtaking only, never turning right
- [ ] **B.** overtaking or turning right
- [ ] **C.** fast-moving traffic only
- [ ] **D.** turning right only, never overtaking

514 You are approaching a busy junction. There are several lanes with road markings. At the last moment you realise that you are in the wrong lane. You should

Mark one answer
- [ ] **A.** continue in that lane
- [ ] **B.** force your way across
- [ ] **C.** stop until the area has cleared
- [ ] **D.** use clear arm signals to cut across

515 Where may you overtake on a one-way street?

Mark one answer
- [ ] **A.** Only on the left-hand side
- [ ] **B.** Overtaking is not allowed
- [ ] **C.** Only on the right-hand side
- [ ] **D.** Either on the right or the left

516 When going straight ahead at a roundabout you should

Mark one answer
- [ ] **A.** indicate left before leaving the roundabout
- [ ] **B.** not indicate at any time
- [ ] **C.** indicate right when approaching the roundabout
- [ ] **D.** indicate left when approaching the roundabout

517 Which vehicle might have to use a different course to normal at roundabouts?

Mark one answer
- [ ] **A.** Sports car
- [ ] **B.** Van
- [ ] **C.** Estate car
- [ ] **D.** Long vehicle

518 You are going straight ahead at a roundabout. How should you signal?

Mark one answer

- A. Signal right on the approach and then left to leave the roundabout
- B. Signal left after you leave the roundabout and enter the new road
- C. Signal right on the approach to the roundabout and keep the signal on
- D. Signal left just after you pass the exit before the one you will take

519 You may only enter a box junction when

Mark one answer

- A. there are less than two vehicles in front of you
- B. the traffic lights show green
- C. your exit road is clear
- D. you need to turn left

520 You may wait in a yellow box junction when

Mark one answer

- A. oncoming traffic is preventing you from turning right
- B. you are in a queue of traffic turning left
- C. you are in a queue of traffic to go ahead
- D. you are on a roundabout

521 You MUST stop when signalled to do so by which THREE of these?

Mark three answers

- A. A police officer
- B. A pedestrian
- C. A school crossing patrol
- D. A bus driver
- E. A red traffic light

522 You will see these red and white markers when approaching

Mark one answer

- A. the end of a motorway
- B. a concealed level crossing
- C. a concealed speed limit sign
- D. the end of a dual carriageway

523 Someone is waiting to cross at a zebra crossing. They are standing on the pavement. You should normally

Mark one answer

- [ ] **A.** go on quickly before they step on to the crossing
- [ ] **B.** stop before you reach the zigzag lines and let them cross
- [ ] **C.** stop, let them cross, wait patiently
- [ ] **D.** ignore them as they are still on the pavement

524 At toucan crossings, apart from pedestrians you should be aware of

Mark one answer

- [ ] **A.** emergency vehicles emerging
- [ ] **B.** buses pulling out
- [ ] **C.** trams crossing in front
- [ ] **D.** cyclists riding across

525 Who can use a toucan crossing?

Mark two answers

- [ ] **A.** Trains
- [ ] **B.** Cyclists
- [ ] **C.** Buses
- [ ] **D.** Pedestrians
- [ ] **E.** Trams

526 At a pelican crossing, what does a flashing amber light mean?

Mark one answer

- [ ] **A.** You must not move off until the lights stop flashing
- [ ] **B.** You must give way to pedestrians still on the crossing
- [ ] **C.** You can move off, even if pedestrians are still on the crossing
- [ ] **D.** You must stop because the lights are about to change to red

527 You are waiting at a pelican crossing. The red light changes to flashing amber. This means you must

Mark one answer

- [ ] **A.** wait for pedestrians on the crossing to clear
- [ ] **B.** move off immediately without any hesitation
- [ ] **C.** wait for the green light before moving off
- [ ] **D.** get ready and go when the continuous amber light shows

528 You are travelling on a well-lit road at night in a built-up area. By using dipped headlights you will be able to

Mark one answer

- [ ] **A.** see further along the road
- [ ] **B.** go at a much faster speed
- [ ] **C.** switch to main beam quickly
- [ ] **D.** be easily seen by others

529 When can you park on the left opposite these road markings?

Mark one answer

- [ ] **A.** If the line nearest to you is broken
- [ ] **B.** When there are no yellow lines
- [ ] **C.** To pick up or set down passengers
- [ ] **D.** During daylight hours only

530
You are intending to turn right at a crossroads. An oncoming driver is also turning right. It will normally be safer to

Mark one answer

A. keep the other vehicle to your RIGHT and turn behind it (offside to offside)
B. keep the other vehicle to your LEFT and turn in front of it (nearside to nearside)
C. carry on and turn at the next junction instead
D. hold back and wait for the other driver to turn first

531
You are on a road that has no traffic signs. There are street lights. What is the speed limit?

Mark one answer

A. 20mph
B. 30mph
C. 40mph
D. 60mph

532
You are going along a street with parked vehicles on the left-hand side. For which THREE reasons should you keep your speed down?

Mark three answers

A. So that oncoming traffic can see you more clearly
B. You may set off car alarms
C. Vehicles may be pulling out
D. Drivers' doors may open
E. Children may run out from between the vehicles

533
You meet an obstruction on your side of the road. You should

Mark one answer

A. carry on, you have priority
B. give way to oncoming traffic
C. wave oncoming vehicles through
D. accelerate to get past first

534
You are on a two-lane dual carriageway. For which TWO of the following would you use the right-hand lane?

Mark two answers

A. Turning right
B. Normal progress
C. Staying at the minimum allowed speed
D. Constant high speed
E. Overtaking slower traffic
F. Mending punctures

535
Who has priority at an unmarked crossroads?

Mark one answer

A. The larger vehicle
B. No one has priority
C. The faster vehicle
D. The smaller vehicle

536
What is the nearest you may park to a junction?

Mark one answer **NI**

A. 10 metres (32 feet)
B. 12 metres (39 feet)
C. 15 metres (49 feet)
D. 20 metres (66 feet)

537
In which THREE places must you NOT park?

Mark three answers **NI**

A. Near the brow of a hill
B. At or near a bus stop
C. Where there is no pavement
D. Within 10 metres (32 feet) of a junction
E. On a 40mph road

538
You are waiting at a level crossing. A train has passed but the lights keep flashing. You must

Mark one answer
- A. carry on waiting
- B. phone the signal operator
- C. edge over the stop line and look for trains
- D. park and investigate

539
You park at night on a road with a 40mph speed limit. You should park

Mark one answer
- A. facing the traffic
- B. with parking lights on
- C. with dipped headlights on
- D. near a street light

540
The dual carriageway you are turning right on to has a very narrow central reservation. What should you do?

Mark one answer
- A. Proceed to the central reservation and wait
- B. Wait until the road is clear in both directions
- C. Stop in the first lane so that other vehicles give way
- D. Emerge slightly to show your intentions

541
At a crossroads there are no signs or road markings. Two vehicles approach. Which has priority?

Mark one answer
- A. Neither of the vehicles
- B. The vehicle travelling the fastest
- C. Oncoming vehicles turning right
- D. Vehicles approaching from the right

542
What does this sign tell you?

Mark one answer
- A. That it is a no-through road
- B. End of traffic calming zone
- C. Free parking zone ends
- D. No waiting zone ends

543
You are entering an area of roadworks. There is a temporary speed limit displayed. You should

Mark one answer
- A. not exceed the speed limit
- B. obey the limit only during rush hour
- C. ignore the displayed limit
- D. obey the limit except at night

544
You are travelling on a motorway. You MUST stop when signalled to do so by which of these?

NI

Mark one answer
- A. Flashing amber lights above your lane
- B. A Highways Agency Traffic Officer
- C. Pedestrians on the hard shoulder
- D. A driver who has broken down

545
At a busy unmarked crossroads, which of the following has priority?

Mark one answer
- A. Vehicles going straight ahead
- B. Vehicles turning right
- C. None of the vehicles
- D. The vehicles that arrived first

546 How should you give an arm signal to turn left?

Mark one answer

A.

B.

C.

D.

547 You are giving an arm signal ready to turn left. Why should you NOT continue with the arm signal while you turn?

Mark one answer

A. Because you might hit a pedestrian on the corner

B. Because you will have less steering control

C. Because you will need to keep the clutch applied

D. Because other motorists will think that you are stopping on the corner

548 This sign is of particular importance to motorcyclists. It means

Mark one answer

A. side winds

B. airport

C. slippery road

D. service area

549 Which one of these signs are you allowed to ride past on a solo motorcycle?

Mark one answer

A.

B.

C.

D.

550 Which of these signals should you give when slowing or stopping your motorcycle?

Mark one answer

A.

B.

C.

D.

551 When drivers flash their headlights at you it means

Mark one answer

- A. that there is a radar speed trap ahead
- B. that they are giving way to you
- C. that they are warning you of their presence
- D. that there is something wrong with your motorcycle

552 You are riding on a motorway. There is a slow-moving vehicle ahead. On the back you see this sign. What should you do?

Mark one answer

- A. Pass on the right
- B. Pass on the left
- C. Leave at the next exit
- D. Drive no further

553 Why should you make sure that you cancel your indicators after turning?

Mark one answer

- A. To avoid flattening the battery
- B. To avoid misleading other road users
- C. To avoid dazzling other road users
- D. To avoid damage to the indicator relay

554 Your indicators are difficult to see due to bright sunshine. When using them you should

Mark one answer

- A. also give an arm signal
- B. sound your horn
- C. flash your headlight
- D. keep both hands on the handlebars

555 You MUST obey signs giving orders. These signs are mostly in

Mark one answer

- A. green rectangles
- B. red triangles
- C. blue rectangles
- D. red circles

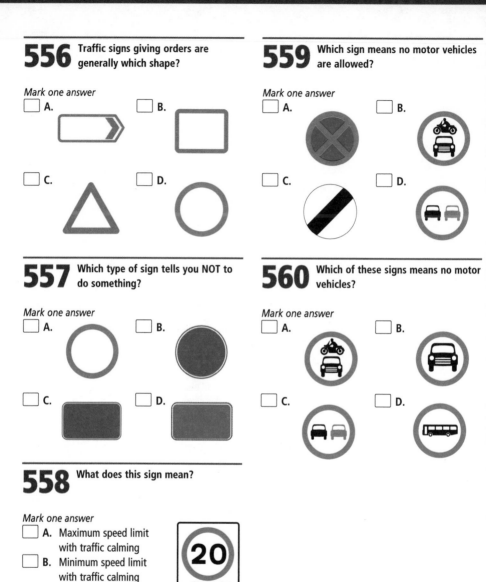

556 Traffic signs giving orders are generally which shape?

Mark one answer

- A.
- B.
- C.
- D.

557 Which type of sign tells you NOT to do something?

Mark one answer

- A.
- B.
- C.
- D.

559 Which sign means no motor vehicles are allowed?

Mark one answer

- A.
- B.
- C.
- D.

560 Which of these signs means no motor vehicles?

Mark one answer

- A.
- B.
- C.
- D.

558 What does this sign mean?

Mark one answer

- A. Maximum speed limit with traffic calming
- B. Minimum speed limit with traffic calming
- C. '20 cars only' parking zone
- D. Only 20 cars allowed at any one time

20 ZONE symbol Place Name

561 What does this sign mean?

Mark one answer
- [ ] **A.** New speed limit 20mph
- [ ] **B.** No vehicles over 30 tonnes
- [ ] **C.** Minimum speed limit 30mph
- [ ] **D.** End of 20mph zone

562 What does this sign mean?

Mark one answer
- [ ] **A.** No overtaking
- [ ] **B.** No motor vehicles
- [ ] **C.** Clearway (no stopping)
- [ ] **D.** Cars and motorcycles only

563 What does this sign mean?

Mark one answer
- [ ] **A.** No parking
- [ ] **B.** No road markings
- [ ] **C.** No through road
- [ ] **D.** No entry

564 What does this sign mean?

Mark one answer
- [ ] **A.** Bend to the right
- [ ] **B.** Road on the right closed
- [ ] **C.** No traffic from the right
- [ ] **D.** No right turn

565 Which sign means 'no entry'?

Mark one answer
- [ ] **A.**
- [ ] **B.**
- [ ] **C.**
- [ ] **D.**

566 What does this sign mean?

Mark one answer

- A. Route for trams only
- B. Route for buses only
- C. Parking for buses only
- D. Parking for trams only

Only

567 Which type of vehicle does this sign apply to?

4.4 m
14'-6"

Mark one answer

- A. Wide vehicles
- B. Long vehicles
- C. High vehicles
- D. Heavy vehicles

568 Which sign means NO motor vehicles allowed?

Mark one answer

- A.
- B.
- C.
- D.

569 What does this sign mean?

Mark one answer

- A. You have priority
- B. No motor vehicles
- C. Two-way traffic
- D. No overtaking

570 What does this sign mean?

Mark one answer

- A. Keep in one lane
- B. Give way to oncoming traffic
- C. Do not overtake
- D. Form two lanes

571 Which sign means no overtaking?

Mark one answer

- [ ] A.
- [ ] B.
- [ ] C.
- [ ] D.

572 What does this sign mean?

Mark one answer

- [ ] A. Waiting restrictions apply
- [ ] B. Waiting permitted
- [ ] C. National speed limit applies
- [ ] D. Clearway (no stopping)

573 What does this sign mean?

Mark one answer

- [ ] A. End of restricted speed area
- [ ] B. End of restricted parking area
- [ ] C. End of clearway
- [ ] D. End of cycle route

Zone
ENDS

574 Which sign means 'no stopping'?

Mark one answer

- [ ] A.
- [ ] B.
- [ ] C.
- [ ] D.

575 What does this sign mean?

Mark one answer

- [ ] A. Roundabout
- [ ] B. Crossroads
- [ ] C. No stopping
- [ ] D. No entry

576 You see this sign ahead. It means

Mark one answer

- [ ] A. national speed limit applies
- [ ] B. waiting restrictions apply
- [ ] C. no stopping
- [ ] D. no entry

577 What does this sign mean?

P

1 mile

Mark one answer
- [ ] **A.** Distance to parking place ahead
- [ ] **B.** Distance to public telephone ahead
- [ ] **C.** Distance to public house ahead
- [ ] **D.** Distance to passing place ahead

578 What does this sign mean?

Mark one answer
- [ ] **A.** Vehicles may not park on the verge or footway
- [ ] **B.** Vehicles may park on the left-hand side of the road only
- [ ] **C.** Vehicles may park fully on the verge or footway
- [ ] **D.** Vehicles may park on the right-hand side of the road only

579 What does this traffic sign mean?

Mark one answer
- [ ] **A.** No overtaking allowed
- [ ] **B.** Give priority to oncoming traffic
- [ ] **C.** Two-way traffic
- [ ] **D.** One-way traffic only

580 What is the meaning of this traffic sign?

Mark one answer
- [ ] **A.** End of two-way road
- [ ] **B.** Give priority to vehicles coming towards you
- [ ] **C.** You have priority over vehicles coming towards you
- [ ] **D.** Bus lane ahead

581 What MUST you do when you see this sign?

Mark one answer
- [ ] **A.** Stop, only if traffic is approaching
- [ ] **B.** Stop, even if the road is clear
- [ ] **C.** Stop, only if children are waiting to cross
- [ ] **D.** Stop, only if a red light is showing

582 What does this sign mean?

Mark one answer
- A. No overtaking
- B. You are entering a one-way street
- C. Two-way traffic ahead
- D. You have priority over vehicles from the opposite direction

583 What shape is a STOP sign at a junction?

Mark one answer
- A.
- B.
- C.
- D.

584 At a junction you see this sign partly covered by snow. What does it mean?

Mark one answer
- A. Crossroads
- B. Give way
- C. Stop
- D. Turn right

585 Which shape is used for a 'give way' sign?

Mark one answer
- A.
- B.
- C.
- D.

586 What does this sign mean?

Mark one answer
- A. Service area 30 miles ahead
- B. Maximum speed 30mph
- C. Minimum speed 30mph
- D. Lay-by 30 miles ahead

587 In some narrow residential streets you may find a speed limit of

Mark one answer
- A. 20mph
- B. 25mph
- C. 35mph
- D. 40mph

588 Which of these signs means turn left ahead?

Mark one answer

A.

B.

C.

D.

589 What does this sign mean?

Mark one answer

A. Buses turning
B. Ring road
C. Mini-roundabout
D. Keep right

590 What does this sign mean?

Mark one answer

A. Give way to oncoming vehicles
B. Approaching traffic passes you on both sides
C. Turn off at the next available junction
D. Pass either side to get to the same destination

591 What does this sign mean?

Mark one answer

A. Route for trams
B. Give way to trams
C. Route for buses
D. Give way to buses

Only

592 What does a circular traffic sign with a blue background do?

Mark one answer

A. Give warning of a motorway ahead
B. Give directions to a car park
C. Give motorway information
D. Give an instruction

593 Which of these signs shows that you are entering a one-way system?

Mark one answer

A.

B.

C.

D.

594 Where would you see a contraflow bus and cycle lane?

Mark one answer

- A. On a dual carriageway
- B. On a roundabout
- C. On an urban motorway
- D. On a one-way street

595 What does this sign mean?

Mark one answer

- A. Bus station on the right
- B. Contraflow bus lane
- C. With-flow bus lane
- D. Give way to buses

596 What does this sign mean?

Mark one answer

- A. With-flow bus and cycle lane
- B. Contraflow bus and cycle lane
- C. No buses and cycles allowed
- D. No waiting for buses and cycles

597 What does a sign with a brown background show?

Mark one answer

- A. Tourist directions
- B. Primary roads
- C. Motorway routes
- D. Minor routes

598 This sign means

Mark one answer

- A. tourist attraction
- B. beware of trains
- C. level crossing
- D. beware of trams

599 What are triangular signs for?

Mark one answer

- **A.** To give warnings
- **B.** To give information
- **C.** To give orders
- **D.** To give directions

600 What does this sign mean?

Mark one answer

- **A.** Turn left ahead
- **B.** T-junction
- **C.** No through road
- **D.** Give way

601 What does this sign mean?

Mark one answer

- **A.** Multi-exit roundabout
- **B.** Risk of ice
- **C.** Six roads converge
- **D.** Place of historical interest

602 What does this sign mean?

Mark one answer

- **A.** Crossroads
- **B.** Level crossing with gate
- **C.** Level crossing without gate
- **D.** Ahead only

603 What does this sign mean?

Mark one answer

- **A.** Ring road
- **B.** Mini-roundabout
- **C.** No vehicles
- **D.** Roundabout

604 Which FOUR of these would be indicated by a triangular road sign?

Mark four answers

- **A.** Road narrows
- **B.** Ahead only
- **C.** Low bridge
- **D.** Minimum speed
- **E.** Children crossing
- **F.** T-junction

605 What does this sign mean?

Mark one answer
- **A.** Cyclists must dismount
- **B.** Cycles are not allowed
- **C.** Cycle route ahead
- **D.** Cycle in single file

606 Which sign means that pedestrians may be walking along the road?

Mark one answer

A.

B.

C.

D.

607 Which of these signs warn you of a zebra crossing?

Mark one answer

A.

B.

C.

D.

608 What does this sign mean?

Mark one answer
- **A.** No footpath ahead
- **B.** Pedestrians only ahead
- **C.** Pedestrian crossing ahead
- **D.** School crossing ahead

609 What does this sign mean?

Mark one answer
- **A.** School crossing patrol
- **B.** No pedestrians allowed
- **C.** Pedestrian zone – no vehicles
- **D.** Zebra crossing ahead

610 Which of these signs means there is a double bend ahead?

Mark one answer

A.

B.

C.

D.

611 What does this sign mean?

Mark one answer

A. Wait at the barriers

B. Wait at the crossroads

C. Give way to trams

D. Give way to farm vehicles

612 What does this sign mean?

Mark one answer

A. Humpback bridge

B. Humps in the road

C. Entrance to tunnel

D. Soft verges

613 What does this sign mean?

Mark one answer

A. Low bridge ahead

B. Tunnel ahead

C. Ancient monument ahead

D. Traffic danger spot ahead

614 What does this sign mean?

Mark one answer

A. Two-way traffic straight ahead

B. Two-way traffic crosses a one-way road

C. Two-way traffic over a bridge

D. Two-way traffic crosses a two-way road

615 Which sign means 'two-way traffic crosses your route ahead'?

Mark one answer

A.

B.

C.

D.

616 Which of these signs means the end of a dual carriageway?

Mark one answer

A.

B.

C.

D.

617 What does this sign mean?

Mark one answer

A. End of dual carriageway

B. Tall bridge

C. Road narrows

D. End of narrow bridge

618 What does this sign mean?

Mark one answer

A. Two-way traffic ahead across a one-way road

B. Traffic approaching you has priority

C. Two-way traffic straight ahead

D. Motorway contraflow system ahead

619 What does this sign mean?

Mark one answer

A. Crosswinds

B. Road noise

C. Airport

D. Adverse camber

620 What does this traffic sign mean?

Mark one answer

A. Slippery road ahead

B. Tyres liable to punctures ahead

C. Danger ahead

D. Service area ahead

621 You are about to overtake when you see this sign. You should

Mark one answer

- [ ] **A.** overtake the other driver as quickly as possible
- [ ] **B.** move to the right to get a better view
- [ ] **C.** switch your headlights on before overtaking
- [ ] **D.** hold back until you can see clearly ahead

Hidden dip

622 What does this sign mean?

Mark one answer

- [ ] **A.** Level crossing with gate or barrier
- [ ] **B.** Gated road ahead
- [ ] **C.** Level crossing without gate or barrier
- [ ] **D.** Cattle grid ahead

623 What does this sign mean?

Mark one answer

- [ ] **A.** No trams ahead
- [ ] **B.** Oncoming trams
- [ ] **C.** Trams crossing ahead
- [ ] **D.** Trams only

624 What does this sign mean?

10%

Mark one answer

- [ ] **A.** Adverse camber
- [ ] **B.** Steep hill downwards
- [ ] **C.** Uneven road
- [ ] **D.** Steep hill upwards

625 What does this sign mean?

Ford

Mark one answer

- [ ] **A.** Uneven road surface
- [ ] **B.** Bridge over the road
- [ ] **C.** Road ahead ends
- [ ] **D.** Water across the road

626 What does this sign mean?

Mark one answer

- [ ] **A.** Humpback bridge
- [ ] **B.** Traffic calming hump
- [ ] **C.** Low bridge
- [ ] **D.** Uneven road

627 What does this sign mean?

Mark one answer
- **A.** Turn left for parking area
- **B.** No through road on the left
- **C.** No entry for traffic turning left
- **D.** Turn left for ferry terminal

628 What does this sign mean?

Mark one answer
- **A.** T-junction
- **B.** No through road
- **C.** Telephone box ahead
- **D.** Toilet ahead

629 Which sign means 'no through road'?

Mark one answer
- **A.**
- **B.** (open circle)
- **C.**
- **D.**

630 Which of the following signs informs you that you are coming to a 'no through road'?

Mark one answer
- **A.**
- **B.**
- **C.**
- **D.**

631 What does this sign mean?

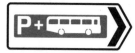

Mark one answer
- **A.** Direction to park-and-ride car park
- **B.** No parking for buses or coaches
- **C.** Directions to bus and coach park
- **D.** Parking area for cars and coaches

632 You are in a tunnel and you see this sign. What does it mean?

Mark one answer
- **A.** Direction to emergency pedestrian exit
- **B.** Beware of pedestrians, no footpath ahead
- **C.** No access for pedestrians
- **D.** Beware of pedestrians crossing ahead

633 Which is the sign for a ring road?

Mark one answer

A.

B.

C.

D.

634 What does this sign mean?

Mark one answer

A. The right-hand lane ahead is narrow

B. Right-hand lane for buses only

C. Right-hand lane for turning right

D. The right-hand lane is closed

635 What does this sign mean?

Mark one answer

A. Change to the left lane

B. Leave at the next exit

C. Contraflow system

D. One-way street

636 At a railway level crossing the red light signal continues to flash after a train has gone by. What should you do?

Mark one answer

A. Phone the signal operator

B. Alert drivers behind you

C. Wait

D. Proceed with caution

637 What does this sign mean?

Mark one answer
- A. Leave motorway at next exit
- B. Lane for heavy and slow vehicles
- C. All lorries use the hard shoulder
- D. Rest area for lorries

638 You are approaching a red traffic light. What will the signal show next?

Mark one answer
- A. Red and amber
- B. Green alone
- C. Amber alone
- D. Green and amber

639 A red traffic light means

Mark one answer
- A. you should stop unless turning left
- B. stop, if you are able to brake safely
- C. you must stop and wait behind the stop line
- D. proceed with caution

640 At traffic lights, amber on its own means

Mark one answer
- A. prepare to go
- B. go if the way is clear
- C. go if no pedestrians are crossing
- D. stop at the stop line

641 You are approaching traffic lights. Red and amber are showing. This means

Mark one answer
- A. pass the lights if the road is clear
- B. there is a fault with the lights – take care
- C. wait for the green light before you cross the stop line
- D. the lights are about to change to red

642
You are at a junction controlled by traffic lights. When should you NOT proceed at green?

Mark one answer

- [ ] A. When pedestrians are waiting to cross
- [ ] B. When your exit from the junction is blocked
- [ ] C. When you think the lights may be about to change
- [ ] D. When you intend to turn right

643
You are in the left-hand lane at traffic lights. You are waiting to turn left. At which of these traffic lights must you NOT move on?

Mark one answer

- [ ] A.
- [ ] B.
- [ ] C.
- [ ] D.

644
What does this sign mean?

Mark one answer

- [ ] A. Traffic lights out of order
- [ ] B. Amber signal out of order
- [ ] C. Temporary traffic lights ahead
- [ ] D. New traffic lights ahead

645
When traffic lights are out of order, who has priority?

Mark one answer

- [ ] A. Traffic going straight on
- [ ] B. Traffic turning right
- [ ] C. Nobody
- [ ] D. Traffic turning left

646
These flashing red lights mean STOP. In which THREE of the following places could you find them?

Mark three answers

- [ ] A. Pelican crossings
- [ ] B. Lifting bridges
- [ ] C. Zebra crossings
- [ ] D. Level crossings
- [ ] E. Motorway exits
- [ ] F. Fire stations

647 What do these zigzag lines at pedestrian crossings mean?

Mark one answer

- **A.** No parking at any time
- **B.** Parking allowed only for a short time
- **C.** Slow down to 20mph
- **D.** Sounding horns is not allowed

648 When may you cross a double solid white line in the middle of the road?

Mark one answer

- **A.** To pass traffic that is queuing back at a junction
- **B.** To pass a car signalling to turn left ahead
- **C.** To pass a road maintenance vehicle travelling at 10mph or less
- **D.** To pass a vehicle that is towing a trailer

649 What does this road marking mean?

Mark one answer

- **A.** Do not cross the line
- **B.** No stopping allowed
- **C.** You are approaching a hazard
- **D.** No overtaking allowed

650 This marking appears on the road just before a

Mark one answer

- **A.** 'no entry' sign
- **B.** 'give way' sign
- **C.** 'stop' sign
- **D.** 'no through road' sign

651 Where would you see this road marking?

Mark one answer

- **A.** At traffic lights
- **B.** On road humps
- **C.** Near a level crossing
- **D.** At a box junction

652 Which is a hazard warning line?

Mark one answer

A.

B.

C.

D.

653

At this junction there is a stop sign with a solid white line on the road surface. Why is there a stop sign here?

Mark one answer

A. Speed on the major road is de-restricted

B. It is a busy junction

C. Visibility along the major road is restricted

D. There are hazard warning lines in the centre of the road

654

You see this line across the road at the entrance to a roundabout. What does it mean?

Mark one answer

A. Give way to traffic from the right

B. Traffic from the left has right of way

C. You have right of way

D. Stop at the line

655 Where would you find these road markings?

Mark one answer

A. At a railway crossing

B. At a junction

C. On a motorway

D. On a pedestrian crossing

656

How will a police officer in a patrol vehicle normally get you to stop?

Mark one answer

A. Flash the headlights, indicate left and point to the left

B. Wait until you stop, then approach you

C. Use the siren, overtake, cut in front and stop

D. Pull alongside you, use the siren and wave you to stop

657 There is a police car following you. The police officer flashes the headlights and points to the left. What should you do?

Mark one answer
- **A.** Turn left at the next junction
- **B.** Pull up on the left
- **C.** Stop immediately
- **D.** Move over to the left

658 You approach a junction. The traffic lights are not working. A police officer gives this signal. You should

Mark one answer
- **A.** turn left only
- **B.** turn right only
- **C.** stop level with the officer's arm
- **D.** stop at the stop line

659 The driver of the car in front is giving this arm signal. What does it mean?

Mark one answer
- **A.** The driver is slowing down
- **B.** The driver intends to turn right
- **C.** The driver wishes to overtake
- **D.** The driver intends to turn left

660 Where would you see these road markings?

Mark one answer
- **A.** At a level crossing
- **B.** On a motorway slip road
- **C.** At a pedestrian crossing
- **D.** On a single-track road

661 What does this motorway sign mean?

Mark one answer
- **A.** Change to the lane on your left
- **B.** Leave the motorway at the next exit
- **C.** Change to the opposite carriageway
- **D.** Pull up on the hard shoulder

662 What does this motorway sign mean?

Mark one answer
- **A.** Temporary minimum speed 50mph
- **B.** No services for 50 miles
- **C.** Obstruction 50 metres (164 feet) ahead
- **D.** Temporary maximum speed 50mph

663 What does this sign mean?

Mark one answer
- A. Through traffic to use left lane
- B. Right-hand lane T-junction only
- C. Right-hand lane closed ahead
- D. 11 tonne weight limit

664 On a motorway this sign means

Mark one answer
- A. move over on to the hard shoulder
- B. overtaking on the left only
- C. leave the motorway at the next exit
- D. move to the lane on your left

665 What does '25' mean on this motorway sign?

Mark one answer
- A. The distance to the nearest town
- B. The route number of the road
- C. The number of the next junction
- D. The speed limit on the slip road

666 The right-hand lane of a three-lane motorway is

Mark one answer
- A. for lorries only
- B. an overtaking lane
- C. the right-turn lane
- D. an acceleration lane

667 Where can you find reflective amber studs on a motorway?

Mark one answer
- A. Separating the slip road from the motorway
- B. On the left-hand edge of the road
- C. On the right-hand edge of the road
- D. Separating the lanes

668 Where on a motorway would you find green reflective studs?

Mark one answer
- A. Separating driving lanes
- B. Between the hard shoulder and the carriageway
- C. At slip road entrances and exits
- D. Between the carriageway and the central reservation

669
You are travelling along a motorway. You see this sign. You should

Mark one answer
- [ ] **A.** leave the motorway at the next exit
- [ ] **B.** turn left immediately
- [ ] **C.** change lane
- [ ] **D.** move onto the hard shoulder

670
At a junction you see this signal. It means

Mark one answer
- [ ] **A.** cars must stop
- [ ] **B.** trams must stop
- [ ] **C.** both trams and cars must stop
- [ ] **D.** both trams and cars can continue

671
What does this sign mean?

Mark one answer
- [ ] **A.** No motor vehicles
- [ ] **B.** End of motorway
- [ ] **C.** No through road
- [ ] **D.** End of bus lane

672
Which of these signs means that the national speed limit applies?

Mark one answer
- [ ] **A.**
- [ ] **B.**
- [ ] **C.**
- [ ] **D.**

673
What is the maximum speed on a single carriageway road?

Mark one answer
- [ ] **A.** 50mph
- [ ] **B.** 60mph
- [ ] **C.** 40mph
- [ ] **D.** 70mph

674
What does this sign mean?

Mark one answer
- [ ] **A.** End of motorway
- [ ] **B.** End of restriction
- [ ] **C.** Lane ends ahead
- [ ] **D.** Free recovery ends

675 This sign is advising you to

Mark one answer
- [ ] **A.** follow the route diversion
- [ ] **B.** follow the signs to the picnic area
- [ ] **C.** give way to pedestrians
- [ ] **D.** give way to cyclists

676 Why would this temporary speed limit sign be shown?

Mark one answer
- [ ] **A.** To warn of the end of the motorway
- [ ] **B.** To warn you of a low bridge
- [ ] **C.** To warn you of a junction ahead
- [ ] **D.** To warn of roadworks ahead

50 ¾ mile ahead

677 This traffic sign means there is

Mark one answer
- [ ] **A.** a compulsory maximum speed limit
- [ ] **B.** an advisory maximum speed limit
- [ ] **C.** a compulsory minimum speed limit
- [ ] **D.** an advised separation distance

678 You see this sign at a crossroads. You should

Mark one answer
- [ ] **A.** maintain the same speed
- [ ] **B.** carry on with great care
- [ ] **C.** find another route
- [ ] **D.** telephone the police

679 You are signalling to turn right in busy traffic. How would you confirm your intention safely?

Mark one answer
- [ ] **A.** Sound the horn
- [ ] **B.** Give an arm signal
- [ ] **C.** Flash your headlights
- [ ] **D.** Position over the centre line

680 What does this sign mean?

Mark one answer
- [ ] **A.** Motorcycles only
- [ ] **B.** No cars
- [ ] **C.** Cars only
- [ ] **D.** No motorcycles

681
You are on a motorway. You see this sign on a lorry that has stopped in the right-hand lane. You should

Mark one answer
- **A.** move into the right-hand lane
- **B.** stop behind the flashing lights
- **C.** pass the lorry on the left
- **D.** leave the motorway at the next exit

682
You are on a motorway. Red flashing lights appear above your lane only. What should you do?

Mark one answer
- **A.** Continue in that lane and look for further information
- **B.** Move into another lane in good time
- **C.** Pull on to the hard shoulder
- **D.** Stop and wait for an instruction to proceed

683
A red traffic light means

Mark one answer
- **A.** you must stop behind the white stop line
- **B.** you may go straight on if there is no other traffic
- **C.** you may turn left if it is safe to do so
- **D.** you must slow down and prepare to stop if traffic has started to cross

684
The driver of this car is giving an arm signal. What are they about to do?

Mark one answer
- **A.** Turn to the right
- **B.** Turn to the left
- **C.** Go straight ahead
- **D.** Let pedestrians cross

685
Which arm signal tells you that the car you are following is going to pull up?

Mark one answer
- **A.**
- **B.**
- **C.**
- **D.**

686
When may you sound the horn?

Mark one answer
- **A.** To give you right of way
- **B.** To attract a friend's attention
- **C.** To warn others of your presence
- **D.** To make slower drivers move over

687 You must not use your horn when you are stationary

Mark one answer

- A. unless a moving vehicle may cause you danger
- B. at any time whatsoever
- C. unless it is used only briefly
- D. except for signalling that you have just arrived

688 What does this sign mean?

URBAN
CLEARWAY
Monday to Friday

am	pm
8.00 - 9.30	4.30 - 6.30

Mark one answer

- A. You can park on the days and times shown
- B. No parking on the days and times shown
- C. No parking at all from Monday to Friday
- D. End of the urban clearway restrictions

689 What does this sign mean?

Mark one answer

- A. Quayside or river bank
- B. Steep hill downwards
- C. Uneven road surface
- D. Road liable to flooding

690 You see this amber traffic light ahead. Which light or lights will come on next?

Mark one answer

- A. Red alone
- B. Red and amber together
- C. Green and amber together
- D. Green alone

691 This broken white line painted in the centre of the road means

Mark one answer

- A. oncoming vehicles have priority over you
- B. you should give priority to oncoming vehicles
- C. there is a hazard ahead of you
- D. the area is a national speed limit zone

692 Which sign means you have priority over oncoming vehicles?

Mark one answer

- A.
- B.
- C.
- D.

693

You see this signal overhead on the motorway. What does it mean?

Mark one answer

- **A.** Leave the motorway at the next exit
- **B.** All vehicles use the hard shoulder
- **C.** Sharp bend to the left ahead
- **D.** Stop, all lanes ahead closed

694

A white line like this along the centre of the road is a

Mark one answer

- **A.** bus lane marking
- **B.** hazard warning
- **C.** give way marking
- **D.** lane marking

695

What is the purpose of these yellow criss-cross lines on the road?

Mark one answer

- **A.** To make you more aware of the traffic lights
- **B.** To guide you into position as you turn
- **C.** To prevent the junction becoming blocked
- **D.** To show you where to stop when the lights change

696

What is the reason for the yellow criss-cross lines painted on the road here?

Mark one answer

- **A.** To mark out an area for trams only
- **B.** To prevent queuing traffic from blocking the junction on the left
- **C.** To mark the entrance lane to a car park
- **D.** To warn you of the tram lines crossing the road

697

What is the reason for the area marked in red and white along the centre of this road?

Mark one answer

- **A.** It is to separate traffic flowing in opposite directions
- **B.** It marks an area to be used by overtaking motorcyclists
- **C.** It is a temporary marking to warn of the roadworks
- **D.** It is separating the two sides of the dual carriageway

698

Other drivers may sometimes flash their headlights at you. In which situation are they allowed to do this?

Mark one answer

- **A.** To warn of a radar speed trap ahead
- **B.** To show that they are giving way to you
- **C.** To warn you of their presence
- **D.** To let you know there is a fault with your vehicle

699

You have just driven past this sign. You should be aware that

Mark one answer

- **A.** it is a single track road
- **B.** you cannot stop on this road
- **C.** there is only one lane in use
- **D.** all traffic is going one way

700

Which sign shows that traffic can only travel in one direction on the road you're on?

Mark one answer

- **A.**
- **B.**
- **C.**
- **D.**

701 You hold a provisional motorcycle licence. This means you must NOT

Mark three answers

- A. exceed 30mph
- B. ride on a motorway
- C. ride after dark
- D. carry a pillion passenger
- E. ride without 'L' plates displayed

702 Which of the following information is found on your motorcycle registration document?

Mark three answers

- A. Make and model
- B. Service history record
- C. Ignition key security number
- D. Engine size and number
- E. Purchase price
- F. Year of first registration

703 A full category A1 licence will allow you to ride a motorcycle up to

Mark one answer

- A. 125cc
- B. 250cc
- C. 350cc
- D. 425cc

704 Compulsory Basic Training (CBT) can only be carried out by

Mark one answer **NI**

- A. any ADI (Approved Driving Instructor)
- B. any road safety officer
- C. any DSA (Driving Standards Agency) approved training body
- D. any motorcycle main dealer

705 Before riding anyone else's motorcycle you should make sure that

Mark one answer

- A. the owner has third party insurance cover
- B. your own motorcycle has insurance cover
- C. the motorcycle is insured for your use
- D. the owner has the insurance documents with them

706 Vehicle excise duty is often called 'Road Tax' or 'The Tax Disc'. You must

Mark one answer

- A. keep it with your registration document
- B. display it clearly on your motorcycle
- C. keep it concealed safely in your motorcycle
- D. carry it on you at all times

707 Motorcycles must FIRST have an MOT test certificate when they are

Mark one answer **NI**

- A. one year old
- B. three years old
- C. five years old
- D. seven years old

708 Which THREE pieces of information are found on a registration document?

Mark three answers

- A. Registered keeper
- B. Make of the motorcycle
- C. Service history details
- D. Date of the MOT
- E. Type of insurance cover
- F. Engine size

709 You have a duty to contact the licensing authority when

Mark three answers

- A. you go abroad on holiday
- B. you change your motorcycle
- C. you change your name
- D. your job status is changed
- E. your permanent address changes
- F. your job involves travelling abroad

710 Your motorcycle is insured third party only. This covers

Mark two answers

- A. damage to your motorcycle
- B. damage to other vehicles
- C. injury to yourself
- D. injury to others
- E. all damage and injury

711 Your motorcycle insurance policy has an excess of £100. What does this mean?

Mark one answer

- A. The insurance company will pay the first £100 of any claim
- B. You will be paid £100 if you do not have a crash
- C. Your motorcycle is insured for a value of £100 if it is stolen
- D. You will have to pay the first £100 of any claim

712 What is the legal minimum insurance cover you must have to ride on public roads?

Mark one answer

- A. Third party, fire and theft
- B. Fully comprehensive
- C. Third party only
- D. Personal injury cover

713 You have a CBT (Compulsory Basic Training) certificate. How long is it valid?

Mark one answer

NI

- A. One year
- B. Two years
- C. Three years
- D. Four years

714 Your road tax is due to expire. To renew it you may need a renewal form, the fee, and valid MOT (if required). What else will you need?

Mark one answer

- A. Proof of purchase receipt
- B. Compulsory Basic Training certificate
- C. A valid certificate of insurance
- D. A complete service record

715 A vehicle registration document will show

Mark one answer

- A. the service history
- B. the year of first registration
- C. the purchase price
- D. the tyre sizes

716 What is the purpose of having a vehicle test certificate (MOT)?

Mark one answer

- A. To make sure your motorcycle is roadworthy
- B. To certify how many miles per gallon it does
- C. To prove you own the motorcycle
- D. To allow you to park in restricted areas

717 You want a licence to ride a large motorcycle via Direct Access. You will

NI

Mark one answer

- A. not require 'L' plates if you have passed a car test
- B. require 'L' plates only when learning on your own machine
- C. require 'L' plates while learning with a qualified instructor
- D. not require 'L' plates if you have passed a moped test

718 Before taking a practical motorcycle test you need

NI

Mark one answer

- A. a full moped licence
- B. a full car licence
- C. a CBT (Compulsory Basic Training) certificate
- D. 12 months riding experience

719 You must notify the licensing authority when

Mark three answers

- A. your health affects your riding
- B. your eyesight does not meet a set standard
- C. you intend lending your motorcycle
- D. your motorcycle requires an MOT certificate
- E. you change your motorcycle

720 You have just passed your practical motorcycle test. This is your first full licence. Within two years you get six penalty points. You will have to

Mark two answers

- A. retake only your theory test
- B. retake your theory and practical tests
- C. retake only your practical test
- D. reapply for your full licence immediately
- E. reapply for your provisional licence

721 A motorcyclist may only carry a pillion passenger when

Mark three answers NI

- [ ] **A.** the rider has successfully completed CBT (Compulsory Basic Training)
- [ ] **B.** the rider holds a full licence for the category of motorcycle
- [ ] **C.** the motorcycle is fitted with rear footrests
- [ ] **D.** the rider has a full car licence and is over 21
- [ ] **E.** there is a proper passenger seat fitted
- [ ] **F.** there is no sidecar fitted to the machine

722 An MOT certificate is normally valid for

Mark one answer

- [ ] **A.** three years after the date it was issued
- [ ] **B.** 10,000 miles
- [ ] **C.** one year after the date it was issued
- [ ] **D.** 30,000 miles

723 A cover note is a document issued before you receive your

Mark one answer

- [ ] **A.** driving licence
- [ ] **B.** insurance certificate
- [ ] **C.** registration document
- [ ] **D.** MOT certificate

724 A police officer asks to see your documents. You do not have them with you. You may be asked to take them to a police station within

Mark one answer

- [ ] **A.** 5 days
- [ ] **B.** 7 days
- [ ] **C.** 14 days
- [ ] **D.** 21 days

725 You have just passed your practical test. You do not hold a full licence in another category. Within two years you get six penalty points on your licence. What will you have to do?

Mark two answers

- [ ] **A.** Retake only your theory test
- [ ] **B.** Retake your theory and practical tests
- [ ] **C.** Retake only your practical test
- [ ] **D.** Reapply for your full licence immediately
- [ ] **E.** Reapply for your provisional licence

726 Your vehicle needs a current MOT certificate. Until you have one you will NOT be able to

Mark one answer

- [ ] **A.** renew your driving licence
- [ ] **B.** change your insurance company
- [ ] **C.** renew your road tax disc
- [ ] **D.** notify a change of address

727 When you apply to renew your Vehicle Excise Duty (tax disc) you must have

Mark one answer

- [ ] **A.** valid insurance
- [ ] **B.** the old tax disc
- [ ] **C.** the handbook
- [ ] **D.** a valid driving licence

728 How long will a Statutory Off Road Notification (SORN) last for?

Mark one answer

- A. 12 months
- B. 24 months
- C. 3 years
- D. 10 years

729 What is a Statutory Off Road Notification (SORN) declaration?

Mark one answer **NI**

- A. A notification to tell VOSA that a vehicle does not have a current MOT
- B. Information kept by the police about the owner of the vehicle
- C. A notification to tell DVLA that a vehicle is not being used on the road
- D. Information held by insurance companies to check the vehicle is insured

730 A Statutory Off Road Notification (SORN) declaration is

Mark one answer **NI**

- A. to tell DVLA that your vehicle is being used on the road but the MOT has expired
- B. to tell DVLA that you no longer own the vehicle
- C. to tell DVLA that your vehicle is not being used on the road
- D. to tell DVLA that you are buying a personal number plate

731 A Statutory Off Road Notification (SORN) is valid

Mark one answer

- A. for as long as the vehicle has an MOT
- B. for 12 months only
- C. only if the vehicle is more than 3 years old
- D. provided the vehicle is insured

732 A Statutory Off Road Notification (SORN) will last

Mark one answer

- A. for the life of the vehicle
- B. for as long as you own the vehicle
- C. for 12 months only
- D. until the vehicle warranty expires

733 What is the maximum specified fine for driving without insurance?

Mark one answer **NI**

- A. £50
- B. £500
- C. £1,000
- D. £5,000

734 When should you update your Vehicle Registration Certificate?

Mark one answer

- A. When you pass your driving test
- B. When you move house
- C. When your vehicle needs an MOT
- D. When you have a collision

735 Who is legally responsible for ensuring that a Vehicle Registration Certificate (V5C) is updated?

Mark one answer

- A. The registered vehicle keeper
- B. The vehicle manufacturer
- C. Your insurance company
- D. The licensing authority

736 You must have valid insurance before you can

Mark one answer

- A. make a SORN declaration
- B. buy or sell a vehicle
- C. apply for a driving licence
- D. obtain a tax disc

737 A friend asks you to give them a lift on your motorcycle. What conditions apply?

Mark one answer

- A. Your motorcycle must be larger than 125cc
- B. You must have three years motorcycle riding experience
- C. The pillion must be a full motorcycle licence-holder
- D. You must have passed your test for a full motorcycle licence

738 For which of these MUST you show your insurance certificate?

Mark one answer

- A. When making a SORN declaration
- B. When buying or selling a vehicle
- C. When a police officer asks you for it
- D. When having an MOT inspection

739 You want to carry a pillion passenger on your motorcycle. To do this

Mark one answer

- A. your motorcycle must be larger than 125cc
- B. they must be a full motorcycle licence-holder
- C. you must have passed your test for a full motorcycle licence
- D. you must have three years motorcycle riding experience

740 Which THREE of these do you need before you can use a vehicle on the road legally?

Mark three answers

- A. A valid driving licence
- B. A valid tax disc clearly displayed
- C. Proof of your identity
- D. Proper insurance cover
- E. Breakdown cover
- F. A vehicle handbook

741 When you apply to renew your vehicle excise licence (tax disc) what must you have?

Mark one answer

- A. Valid insurance
- B. The old tax disc
- C. The vehicle handbook
- D. A valid driving licence

742 Your motorcycle has broken down on a motorway. How will you know the direction of the nearest emergency telephone?

Mark one answer
- [ ] **A.** By walking with the flow of traffic
- [ ] **B.** By following an arrow on a marker post
- [ ] **C.** By walking against the flow of traffic
- [ ] **D.** By remembering where the last phone was

743 You are travelling on a motorway. A bag falls from your motorcycle. There are valuables in the bag. What should you do?

Mark one answer
- [ ] **A.** Go back carefully and collect the bag as quickly as possible
- [ ] **B.** Stop wherever you are and pick up the bag, but only when there is a safe gap
- [ ] **C.** Stop on the hard shoulder and use the emergency telephone to inform the authorities
- [ ] **D.** Stop on the hard shoulder and then retrieve the bag yourself

744 You should use the engine cut-out switch to

Mark one answer
- [ ] **A.** stop the engine in an emergency
- [ ] **B.** stop the engine on short journeys
- [ ] **C.** save wear on the ignition switch
- [ ] **D.** start the engine if you lose the key

745 You are riding on a motorway. The car in front switches on its hazard warning lights whilst moving. This means

Mark one answer
- [ ] **A.** they are going to take the next exit
- [ ] **B.** there is a danger ahead
- [ ] **C.** there is a police car in the left lane
- [ ] **D.** they are trying to change lanes

746 You are on the motorway. Luggage falls from your motorcycle. What should you do?

Mark one answer
- [ ] **A.** Stop at the next emergency telephone and report the hazard
- [ ] **B.** Stop on the motorway and put on hazard lights while you pick it up
- [ ] **C.** Walk back up the motorway to pick it up
- [ ] **D.** Pull up on the hard shoulder and wave traffic down

747 You are in collision with another vehicle. Someone is injured. Your motorcycle is damaged. Which FOUR of the following should you find out?

Mark four answers
- [ ] **A.** Whether the driver owns the other vehicle involved
- [ ] **B.** The other driver's name, address and telephone number
- [ ] **C.** The make and registration number of the other vehicle
- [ ] **D.** The occupation of the other driver
- [ ] **E.** The details of the other driver's vehicle insurance
- [ ] **F.** Whether the other driver is licensed to drive

748 You have broken down on a motorway. When you use the emergency telephone you will be asked

Mark three answers

- A. for the number on the telephone that you are using
- B. for your driving licence details
- C. for the name of your vehicle insurance company
- D. for details of yourself and your motorcycle
- E. whether you belong to a motoring organisation

749 You are on a motorway. When can you use hazard warning lights?

Mark one answer

- A. When a vehicle is following too closely
- B. When you slow down quickly because of danger ahead
- C. When you are being towed by another vehicle
- D. When riding on the hard shoulder

750 Your motorcycle breaks down in a tunnel. What should you do?

Mark one answer

- A. Stay with your motorcycle and wait for the police
- B. Stand in the lane behind your motorcycle to warn others
- C. Stand in front of your motorcycle to warn oncoming drivers
- D. Switch on hazard lights then go and call for help immediately

751 You are riding through a tunnel. Your motorcycle breaks down. What should you do?

Mark one answer

- A. Switch on hazard warning lights
- B. Remain on your motorcycle
- C. Wait for the police to find you
- D. Rely on CCTV cameras seeing you

752 At the scene of a traffic incident you should

Mark one answer

- A. not put yourself at risk
- B. go to those casualties who are screaming
- C. pull everybody out of their vehicles
- D. leave vehicle engines switched on

753 You are the first to arrive at the scene of a crash. Which TWO of these should you do?

Mark two answers

- A. Leave as soon as another motorist arrives
- B. Make sure engines are switched off
- C. Drag all casualties away from the vehicle(s)
- D. Call the emergency services promptly

754 A collision has just happened. An injured person is lying in a busy road. What is the FIRST thing you should do to help?

Mark one answer

- A. Treat the person for shock
- B. Warn other traffic
- C. Place them in the recovery position
- D. Make sure the injured person is kept warm

755 You are the first person to arrive at an incident where people are badly injured. Which THREE should you do?

Mark three answers

- **A.** Switch on your own hazard warning lights
- **B.** Make sure that someone telephones for an ambulance
- **C.** Try and get people who are injured to drink something
- **D.** Move the people who are injured clear of their vehicles
- **E.** Get people who are not injured clear of the scene

756 You arrive at the scene of a motorcycle crash. The rider is injured. When should the helmet be removed?

Mark one answer

- **A.** Only when it is essential
- **B.** Always straight away
- **C.** Only when the motorcyclist asks
- **D.** Always, unless they are in shock

757 You arrive at a serious motorcycle crash. The motorcyclist is unconscious and bleeding. Your THREE main priorities should be to

Mark three answers

- **A.** try to stop the bleeding
- **B.** make a list of witnesses
- **C.** check their breathing
- **D.** take the numbers of other vehicles
- **E.** sweep up any loose debris
- **F.** check their airways

758 You arrive at an incident. A motorcyclist is unconscious. Your FIRST priority is the casualty's

Mark one answer

- **A.** breathing
- **B.** bleeding
- **C.** broken bones
- **D.** bruising

759 At an incident a casualty is unconscious. Which THREE of these should you check urgently?

Mark three answers

- **A.** Circulation
- **B.** Airway
- **C.** Shock
- **D.** Breathing
- **E.** Broken bones

760 You arrive at the scene of an incident. It has just happened and someone is unconscious. Which THREE of these should be given urgent priority to help them?

Mark three answers

- **A.** Clear the airway and keep it open
- **B.** Try to get them to drink water
- **C.** Check that they are breathing
- **D.** Look for any witnesses
- **E.** Stop any heavy bleeding
- **F.** Take the numbers of vehicles involved

761 At an incident someone is unconscious. Your THREE main priorities should be to

Mark three answers

- **A.** sweep up the broken glass
- **B.** take the names of witnesses
- **C.** count the number of vehicles involved
- **D.** check the airway is clear
- **E.** make sure they are breathing
- **F.** stop any heavy bleeding

762 You have stopped at an incident to give help. Which THREE things should you do?

Mark three answers

- A. Keep injured people warm and comfortable
- B. Keep injured people calm by talking to them reassuringly
- C. Keep injured people on the move by walking them around
- D. Give injured people a warm drink
- E. Make sure that injured people are not left alone

763 You arrive at an incident. It has just happened and someone is injured. Which THREE should be given urgent priority?

Mark three answers

- A. Stop any severe bleeding
- B. Give them a warm drink
- C. Check they are breathing
- D. Take numbers of vehicles involved
- E. Look for witnesses
- F. Clear their airway and keep it open

764 At an incident a casualty has stopped breathing. You should

Mark two answers

- A. remove anything that is blocking the mouth
- B. keep the head tilted forwards as far as possible
- C. raise the legs to help with circulation
- D. try to give the casualty something to drink
- E. tilt the head back gently to clear the airway

765 You are at the scene of an incident. Someone is suffering from shock. You should

Mark four answers

- A. reassure them constantly
- B. offer them a cigarette
- C. keep them warm
- D. avoid moving them if possible
- E. avoid leaving them alone
- F. give them a warm drink

766 Which of the following should you NOT do at the scene of a collision?

Mark one answer

- A. Warn other traffic by switching on your hazard warning lights
- B. Call the emergency services immediately
- C. Offer someone a cigarette to calm them down
- D. Ask drivers to switch off their engines

767 There has been a collision. A driver is suffering from shock. What TWO of these should you do?

Mark two answers

- A. Give them a drink
- B. Reassure them
- C. Not leave them alone
- D. Offer them a cigarette
- E. Ask who caused the incident

768 You have to treat someone for shock at the scene of an incident. You should

Mark one answer

- A. reassure them constantly
- B. walk them around to calm them down
- C. give them something cold to drink
- D. cool them down as soon as possible

769

You arrive at the scene of a motorcycle crash. No other vehicle is involved. The rider is unconscious and lying in the middle of the road. The FIRST thing you should do is

Mark one answer

- A. move the rider out of the road
- B. warn other traffic
- C. clear the road of debris
- D. give the rider reassurance

770

At an incident a small child is not breathing. To restore normal breathing you should breathe into their mouth

Mark one answer

- A. sharply
- B. gently
- C. heavily
- D. rapidly

771

At an incident a casualty is not breathing. To start the process to restore normal breathing you should

Mark three answers

- A. tilt their head forward
- B. clear the airway
- C. turn them on their side
- D. tilt their head back gently
- E. pinch the nostrils together
- F. put their arms across their chest

772

You arrive at the scene of an incident There has been an engine fire and someone's hands and arms have been burnt. You should NOT

Mark one answer

- A. douse the burn thoroughly with clean cool non-toxic liquid
- B. lay the casualty down on the ground
- C. remove anything sticking to the burn
- D. reassure them confidently and repeatedly

773

You arrive at an incident where someone is suffering from severe burns. You should

Mark one answer

- A. apply lotions to the injury
- B. burst any blisters
- C. remove anything stuck to the burns
- D. douse the burns with clean cool non-toxic liquid

774

You arrive at an incident. A pedestrian has a severe bleeding leg wound. It is not broken and there is nothing in the wound. What TWO of these should you do?

Mark two answers

- A. Dab the wound to stop bleeding
- B. Keep both legs flat on the ground
- C. Apply firm pressure to the wound
- D. Raise the leg to lessen bleeding
- E. Fetch them a warm drink

775 You arrive at the scene of a crash. Someone is bleeding badly from an arm wound. There is nothing embedded in it. What should you do?

Mark one answer

- **A.** Apply pressure over the wound and keep the arm down
- **B.** Dab the wound
- **C.** Get them a drink
- **D.** Apply pressure over the wound and raise the arm

776 At an incident a casualty is unconscious but still breathing. You should only move them if

Mark one answer

- **A.** an ambulance is on its way
- **B.** bystanders advise you to
- **C.** there is further danger
- **D.** bystanders will help you to

777 At a collision you suspect a casualty has back injuries. The area is safe. You should

Mark one answer

- **A.** offer them a drink
- **B.** not move them
- **C.** raise their legs
- **D.** not call an ambulance

778 At an accident it is important to look after any casualties. When the area is safe, you should

Mark one answer

- **A.** get them out of the vehicle
- **B.** give them a drink
- **C.** give them something to eat
- **D.** keep them in the vehicle

779 A tanker is involved in a collision. Which sign shows that it is carrying dangerous goods?

Mark one answer

- **A.** LONG VEHICLE
- **B.** 2YE 1089
- **C.**
- **D.**

780 You are involved in a collision. Because of this which THREE of these documents may the police ask you to produce?

Mark three answers

- **A.** Vehicle registration document
- **B.** Driving licence
- **C.** Theory test certificate
- **D.** Insurance certificate
- **E.** MOT test certificate
- **F.** Vehicle service record

781 You see a car on the hard shoulder of a motorway with a HELP pennant displayed. This means the driver is most likely to be

Mark one answer
- [ ] **A.** a disabled person
- [ ] **B.** first aid trained
- [ ] **C.** a foreign visitor
- [ ] **D.** a rescue patrol person

782 On the motorway, the hard shoulder should be used

Mark one answer
- [ ] **A.** to answer a mobile phone
- [ ] **B.** when an emergency arises
- [ ] **C.** for a short rest when tired
- [ ] **D.** to check a road atlas

783 For which TWO should you use hazard warning lights?

Mark two answers
- [ ] **A.** When you slow down quickly on a motorway because of a hazard ahead
- [ ] **B.** When you have broken down
- [ ] **C.** When you wish to stop on double yellow lines
- [ ] **D.** When you need to park on the pavement

784 When are you allowed to use hazard warning lights?

Mark one answer
- [ ] **A.** When stopped and temporarily obstructing traffic
- [ ] **B.** When travelling during darkness without headlights
- [ ] **C.** When parked for shopping on double yellow lines
- [ ] **D.** When travelling slowly because you are lost

785 You are on a motorway. A large box falls onto the road from a lorry. The lorry does not stop. You should

Mark one answer
- [ ] **A.** go to the next emergency telephone and report the hazard
- [ ] **B.** catch up with the lorry and try to get the driver's attention
- [ ] **C.** stop close to the box until the police arrive
- [ ] **D.** pull over to the hard shoulder, then remove the box

786 There has been a collision. A motorcyclist is lying injured and unconscious. Unless it's essential, why should you usually NOT attempt to remove their helmet?

Mark one answer
- [ ] **A.** Because they may not want you to
- [ ] **B.** This could result in more serious injury
- [ ] **C.** They will get too cold if you do this
- [ ] **D.** Because you could scratch the helmet

787 After a collision, someone is unconscious in their vehicle. When should you call the emergency services?

Mark one answer

- **A.** Only as a last resort
- **B.** As soon as possible
- **C.** After you have woken them up
- **D.** After checking for broken bones

788 A casualty has an injured arm. They can move it freely, but it is bleeding. Why should you get them to keep it in a raised position?

Mark one answer

- **A.** Because it will ease the pain
- **B.** It will help them to be seen more easily
- **C.** To stop them touching other people
- **D.** It will help to reduce the blood flow

789 You are going through a congested tunnel and have to stop. What should you do?

Mark one answer

- **A.** Pull up very close to the vehicle in front to save space
- **B.** Ignore any message signs as they are never up to date
- **C.** Keep a safe distance from the vehicle in front
- **D.** Make a U-turn and find another route

790 You are going through a long tunnel. What will warn you of congestion or an incident ahead?

Mark one answer

- **A.** Hazard warning lines
- **B.** Other drivers flashing their lights
- **C.** Variable message signs
- **D.** Areas marked with hatch markings

791 You are going through a tunnel. What systems are provided to warn of any incidents, collisions or congestion?

Mark one answer

- **A.** Double white centre lines
- **B.** Variable message signs
- **C.** Chevron 'distance markers'
- **D.** Rumble strips

792 You are at an incident where a casualty is unconscious. Their breathing should be checked. This should be done for at least

Mark one answer

- **A.** 2 seconds
- **B.** 10 seconds
- **C.** 1 minute
- **D.** 2 minutes

793 Following a collision someone has suffered a burn. The burn needs to be cooled. What is the shortest time it should be cooled for?

Mark one answer

- **A.** 5 minutes
- **B.** 10 minutes
- **C.** 15 minutes
- **D.** 20 minutes

794 After a collision someone has suffered a burn. The burn needs to be cooled. What is the shortest time it should be cooled for?

Mark one answer
- **A.** 30 seconds
- **B.** 60 seconds
- **C.** 5 minutes
- **D.** 10 minutes

795 A casualty is not breathing normally. Chest compressions should be given. At what rate?

Mark one answer
- **A.** 50 per minute
- **B.** 100 per minute
- **C.** 200 per minute
- **D.** 250 per minute

796 An adult casualty is not breathing. To maintain circulation, compressions should be given. What is the correct depth to press?

Mark one answer
- **A.** 1 to 2 centimetres
- **B.** 4 to 5 centimetres
- **C.** 10 to 15 centimetres
- **D.** 15 to 20 centimetres

797 A person has been injured. They may be suffering from shock. What are the warning signs to look for?

Mark one answer
- **A.** Flushed complexion
- **B.** Warm dry skin
- **C.** Slow pulse
- **D.** Pale grey skin

798 You suspect that an injured person may be suffering from shock. What are the warning signs to look for?

Mark one answer
- **A.** Warm dry skin
- **B.** Sweating
- **C.** Slow pulse
- **D.** Skin rash

799 An injured person has been placed in the recovery position. They are unconscious but breathing normally. What else should be done?

Mark one answer
- **A.** Press firmly between the shoulders
- **B.** Place their arms by their side
- **C.** Give them a hot sweet drink
- **D.** Check the airway is clear

800 An injured motorcyclist is lying unconscious in the road. You should always

Mark one answer
- **A.** remove the safety helmet
- **B.** Seek medical assistance
- **C.** move the person off the road
- **D.** remove the leather jacket

801 If a trailer swerves or snakes when you are towing it you should

Mark one answer

- [ ] A. ease off the throttle and reduce your speed
- [ ] B. let go of the handlebars and let it correct itself
- [ ] C. brake hard and hold the brake on
- [ ] D. increase your speed as quickly as possible

802 When riding with a sidecar attached for the first time you should

Mark two answers

- [ ] A. keep your speed down
- [ ] B. be able to stop more quickly
- [ ] C. accelerate quickly round bends
- [ ] D. approach corners more carefully

803 You hold a provisional motorcycle licence. Are you allowed to carry a pillion passenger?

Mark one answer

- [ ] A. Only if the passenger holds a full licence
- [ ] B. Not at any time
- [ ] C. Not unless you are undergoing training
- [ ] D. Only if the passenger is under 21

804 Which THREE must a learner motorcyclist under 21 NOT do?

Mark three answers

- [ ] A. Ride a motorcycle with an engine capacity greater than 125cc
- [ ] B. Pull a trailer
- [ ] C. Carry a pillion passenger
- [ ] D. Ride faster than 30mph
- [ ] E. Use the right-hand lane on dual carriageways

805 When carrying extra weight on a motorcycle, you may need to make adjustments to the

Mark three answers

- [ ] A. headlight
- [ ] B. gears
- [ ] C. suspension
- [ ] D. tyres
- [ ] E. footrests

806 To obtain the full category 'A' licence through the accelerated or direct access scheme, your motorcycle must be

NI

Mark one answer

- [ ] A. solo with maximum power 25kw (33bhp)
- [ ] B. solo with maximum power of 11kw (14.6bhp)
- [ ] C. fitted with a sidecar and have minimum power of 35kw (46.6bhp)
- [ ] D. solo with minimum power of 35kw (46.6bhp)

807 Any load that is carried on a luggage rack MUST be

Mark one answer

- [ ] A. securely fastened when riding
- [ ] B. carried only when strictly necessary
- [ ] C. visible when you are riding
- [ ] D. covered with plastic sheeting

808 Pillion passengers should

Mark one answer

- **A.** have a provisional motorcycle licence
- **B.** be lighter than the rider
- **C.** always wear a helmet
- **D.** signal for the rider

809 Pillion passengers should

Mark one answer

- **A.** give the rider directions
- **B.** lean with the rider when going round bends
- **C.** check the road behind for the rider
- **D.** give arm signals for the rider

810 When you are going around a corner your pillion passenger should

Mark one answer

- **A.** give arm signals for you
- **B.** check behind for other vehicles
- **C.** lean with you on bends
- **D.** lean to one side to see ahead

811 Which of these may need to be adjusted when carrying a pillion passenger?

Mark one answer

- **A.** Indicators
- **B.** Exhaust
- **C.** Fairing
- **D.** Headlight

812 You are towing a trailer with your motorcycle. You should remember that your

Mark one answer

- **A.** stopping distance may increase
- **B.** fuel consumption will improve
- **C.** tyre grip will increase
- **D.** stability will improve

813 Carrying a heavy load in your top box may

Mark one answer

- **A.** cause high-speed weave
- **B.** cause a puncture
- **C.** use less fuel
- **D.** improve stability

814 Heavy loads in a motorcycle top box may

Mark one answer

- A. improve stability
- B. cause low-speed wobble
- C. cause a puncture
- D. improve braking

815 You want to tow a trailer behind your motorcycle. You should

Mark two answers

- A. display a 'long vehicle' sign
- B. fit a larger battery
- C. have a full motorcycle licence
- D. ensure that your engine is more than 125cc
- E. ensure that your motorcycle has shaft drive

816 Overloading your motorcycle can seriously affect the

Mark one answer

- A. gearbox
- B. weather protection
- C. handling
- D. battery life

817 Who is responsible for making sure that a motorcycle is not overloaded?

Mark one answer

- A. The rider of the motorcycle
- B. The owner of the items being carried
- C. The licensing authority
- D. The owner of the motorcycle

818 Before fitting a sidecar to a motorcycle you should

Mark one answer

- A. have the wheels balanced
- B. have the engine tuned
- C. pass the extended bike test
- D. check that the motorcycle is suitable

819 You are using throwover saddlebags. Why is it important to make sure they are evenly loaded?

Mark one answer

- A. They will be uncomfortable for you to sit on
- B. They will slow your motorcycle down
- C. They could make your motorcycle unstable
- D. They will be uncomfortable for a pillion passenger to sit on

820 You are carrying a bulky tank bag. What could this affect?

Mark one answer

- A. Your ability to steer
- B. Your ability to accelerate
- C. Your view ahead
- D. Your insurance premium

821
To carry a pillion passenger you must

Mark one answer

- **A.** hold a full car licence
- **B.** hold a full motorcycle licence
- **C.** be over the age of 21
- **D.** be over the age of 25

822
When carrying a heavy load on your luggage rack, you may need to adjust your

Mark one answer

- **A.** carburettor
- **B.** fuel tap
- **C.** seating position
- **D.** tyre pressures

823
You are carrying a pillion passenger. When following other traffic, which of the following should you do?

Mark one answer

- **A.** Keep to your normal following distance
- **B.** Get your passenger to keep checking behind
- **C.** Keep further back than you normally would
- **D.** Get your passenger to signal for you

824
You should only carry a child as a pillion passenger when

Mark one answer

- **A.** they are over 14 years old
- **B.** they are over 16 years old
- **C.** they can reach the floor from the seat
- **D.** they can reach the handholds and footrests

825
You have fitted a sidecar to your motorcycle. You should make sure that the sidecar

Mark one answer

- **A.** has a registration plate
- **B.** is correctly aligned
- **C.** has a waterproof cover
- **D.** has a solid cover

826
You are riding a motorcycle and sidecar. The extra weight

Mark one answer

- **A.** will allow you to corner more quickly
- **B.** will allow you to brake later for hazards
- **C.** may increase your stopping distance
- **D.** will improve your fuel consumption

827
You are carrying a pillion passenger. To allow for the extra weight which of the following is most likely to need adjustment?

Mark one answer

- **A.** Preload on the front forks
- **B.** Preload on the rear shock absorber(s)
- **C.** The balance of the rear wheel
- **D.** The front and rear wheel alignment

828
A trailer on a motorcycle must be no wider than

Mark one answer

- **A.** 0.5 metres (1 foot 8 inches)
- **B.** 1 metre (3 feet 3 inches)
- **C.** 1.5 metres (4 feet 11 inches)
- **D.** 2 metres (6 feet 6 inches)

829 To carry a pillion passenger your motorcycle should be fitted with

Mark two answers
- A. rear footrests
- B. an engine of 250cc or over
- C. a top box
- D. a grab handle
- E. a proper pillion seat

830 You want to tow a trailer with your motorcycle. Which one applies?

Mark one answer
- A. The motorcycle should be attached to a sidecar
- B. The trailer should weigh more than the motorcycle
- C. The trailer should be fitted with brakes
- D. The trailer should NOT be more than 1 metre (3 feet 3 inches) wide

831 Your motorcycle is fitted with a top box. It is unwise to carry a heavy load in the top box because it may

Mark three answers
- A. reduce stability
- B. improve stability
- C. make turning easier
- D. cause high-speed weave
- E. cause low-speed wobble
- F. increase fuel economy

832 You have a sidecar fitted to your motorcycle. What effect will it have?

Mark one answer
- A. Reduce stability
- B. Make steering lighter
- C. Increase stopping distance
- D. Increase fuel economy

833 You are towing a small trailer on a busy three-lane motorway. All the lanes are open. You must

Mark two answers
- A. not exceed 60mph
- B. not overtake
- C. have a stabiliser fitted
- D. use only the left and centre lanes

Glossary

Accelerate
To make the motorcycle move faster.

Advanced stop lines
A marked area on the road at traffic lights, which permits cyclists or buses to wait in front of other traffic.

Adverse weather
Bad weather that makes riding difficult or dangerous.

Alert
A state of mind in which you are quick to notice possible hazards.

Anticipation
Looking out for hazards and taking action before a problem starts.

Anti-lock brakes (ABS)
Brakes that stop the wheels locking so that you are less likely to skid on a slippery road.

Aquaplane
To slide out of control on a waterlogged road surface because a film of water has built up between your tyres and the road, and your tyres are unable to grip the road.

Articulated vehicle
A long vehicle that is divided into two or more sections connected by joints.

Attitude
The way you think or feel, which affects the way you drive. Especially, whether you are patient and polite, or impatient and aggressive.

Awareness
Taking notice of the road and traffic conditions around you at all times when you are riding.

Black ice
An invisible film of ice that forms over the road surface, creating very dangerous riding conditions.

Blind spot
The section of road behind you which you cannot see in your mirrors. You 'cover' your blind spot by looking over your shoulder before moving off, cornering or overtaking.

Brake fade
Loss of power to the brakes when you have been using them for a long time. For example, when riding down a steep hill. The brakes will overheat and not work properly.

Braking distance
The distance you must allow to slow the motorcycle in order to come to a stop.

Brow
The highest point of a hill.

Built-up area
A town, or place with lots of buildings.

Carriageway
One side of a road or motorway. A 'dual carriageway' has two lanes on each side of a central reservation.

Catalytic converter
A piece of equipment fitted in the exhaust system that changes harmful gases into less harmful ones.

Centre stand
An alternative to a side stand, which gives the motorcycle more stability when parked. Also useful for carrying out maintenance checks.

Chicane
A road sign designed to warn road users to slow down because a sharp double bend is coming up on the road ahead.

Choke
Often manual on a motorcycle.

Clearway
A road where no stopping is allowed at any time. The sign for a clearway is a red cross in a red circle on a blue background.

Commentary riding
Talking to yourself about what you see on the road ahead and what action you are going to take – an aid to concentration.

Comprehensive insurance
A motorcycle insurance policy that pays for repairs even if you cause an accident.

Concentration
Keeping all your attention on your riding.

Conditions

How good or bad the road surface is, volume of traffic on the road, and what the weather is like.

Congestion

Heavy traffic that makes it difficult to get to where you want to go.

Consideration

Thinking about other road users and not just yourself. For example, letting another driver go first at a junction, or stopping at a zebra crossing to let pedestrians cross over.

Compulsory Basic Training (CBT)

A one-day training course of predominantly practical training that, when successfully completed, entitles the CBT certificate holder to ride a motorcycle up to 125cc (50cc for 16-year -olds) on the road with 'L' Plates. The certificate is valid for two years but riders are not allowed to carry pillion passengers or ride on motorways.

Contraflow

When traffic on a motorway follows signs to move to the opposite carriageway for a short distance because of roadworks. (During a contraflow, there is traffic driving in both directions on the same side of the motorway.)

Defensive riding

Riding in such a way as to create a safe zone around yourself. Anticipating hazards and the actions of other drivers and keeping yourself safe while riding.

Disqualified

Stopped from doing something (e.g. riding) by law, because you have broken the law.

Distraction

Anything that stops you concentrating on your riding and the other road users around you.

Document

An official paper or card, for example your motorcycle licence.

Drive chain

The chain between the engine and the rear-wheel. A poorly adjusted drive chain can cause unpredictable acceleration, fall off or even snap causing injury to the rider or a road accident.

Dual carriageway

One side of a road or motorway, with two lanes on each side of a central reservation.

Engine braking – see also gears

Using the low gears to keep your speed down. For example, when you are riding down a steep hill and you want to stop the motorcycle running away. Using the gears instead of braking will help to prevent brake fade.

Engine cut-out switch

A switch, which is designed to stop the engine in an emergency, for example after a road accident, to prevent fire.

Environment

The world around us and the air we breathe.

Exceed

Go higher than an upper limit.

Exhaust emissions

Gases that come out of the exhaust pipe to form part of the outside air.

Field of vision

How far you can see in front and around you when you are riding.

Filler cap

Provides access to the motorcycle's fuel tank, for filling up with petrol or diesel.

Fog lights

Extra bright rear (and sometimes front) lights which may be switched on in conditions of very poor visibility. You must remember to switch them off when visibility improves, as they can dazzle and distract other road users.

Ford

A place in a stream or river which is shallow enough to ride across with care.

Frustration

Feeling annoyed because you cannot ride as fast as you want to because of other drivers or heavy traffic.

Fuel consumption

The amount of fuel that your motorcycle uses. Different motorcycles have different rates of consumption. Increased fuel consumption means using more fuel. Decreased fuel consumption means using less fuel.

Fuel gauge

A display or dial on the instrument panel that tells you how much fuel (petrol or diesel) you have left.

Gantry

An overhead platform like a high narrow bridge that displays electric signs on a motorway.

Gears

Control the speed of the engine in relation to the motorcycle's speed. In a low gear (such as first or second) the engine runs more slowly. In a high gear (such as fourth or fifth), it runs more quickly. Putting the motorcycle into a lower gear as you drive can create the effect of engine braking – forcing the engine to run more slowly.

Handling

How well your motorcycle moves or responds when you steer or brake.

Harass

To ride in a way that makes other road users afraid.

Hard shoulder

The single lane to the left of the inside lane on a motorway, which is for emergency use only. You should not ride on the hard shoulder except in an emergency, or when there are signs telling you to use the hard shoulder because of roadworks.

Harsh braking (or harsh acceleration)

Using the brake or accelerator too hard so as to cause wear on the engine.

Hazard warning lights

Flashing amber lights which warn you that a vehicle has broken down. Your hazard warning lights should only be used to warn other traffic that you have broken down. On a motorway you can use them to warn other road users behind of a hazard ahead.

High-sided vehicle

A van or truck with tall sides, or a tall trailer such as a caravan or horse-box, that is at risk of being blown off-course in strong winds.

The Highway Code

Essential reading for everyone, not just learners, the Highway Code sets out the rules and regulations for all road-users.

Impatient

Not wanting to wait for pedestrians and other road users.

Indicator

Often referred to as a 'signal' in motorcycling.

Inflate

To blow up – to put air in your tyres until they are at the right pressures.

Instrument panel

The motorcycle's electrical controls and gauges.

Intimidate

To make someone feel afraid.

Involved

Being part of something. For example, being one of the riders in an accident.

Jump leads

A pair of thick electric cables with clips at either end. You use it to charge a flat battery by connecting it to the live battery in another vehicle.

Junction

A place where two or more roads join.

Liability

Being legally responsible.

Lifesaver

Called a lifesaver for good reason, this is the final rearward glance that a rider should give before making any manoeuvre. Forgetting to give a lifesaver could cause you to lose yours.

Manoeuvre

Using the controls to make your motorcycle move in a particular direction. For example cornering or parking.

Maximum

Maximum means greatest so, the 'maximum speed' is the highest speed allowed.

Minimum

The smallest possible.

Mobility

The ability to move around easily.

Monotonous

Boring, for example, a long stretch of motorway with no variety and nothing interesting to see.

MOT

The test that proves your motorcycle is safe to drive. Your MOT certificate is one of the important documents for your motorcycle.

Motorway

A fast road that has two or more lanes on each side and a hard shoulder. Riders must join or leave it on the left, via a motorway junction. Many kinds of slower vehicles – such as bicycles – are not allowed on motorways.

Multiple-choice questions

Questions with several possible answers where you have to try to choose the right one/s.

Observation

The ability to notice important information, such as hazards developing ahead. The term 'observation' is often used an alternative to 'lifesaver'.

Obstruct

To get in the way of another road user.

Octagonal

Having eight sides.

Oil level

The amount of oil that is in the engine. The oil level should be checked as part of your regular maintenance routine, and the oil topped up or replaced as necessary. The engine cannot run effectively and may be damaged if the oil level is too low.

Pedestrian

A person walking.

Pegasus crossing

An unusual kind of crossing. It has a button high up for horse riders to push. (Pegasus was a flying horse in Greek legend.)

Pelican crossing

A crossing with traffic lights that pedestrians can use by pushing a button. Vehicles must give way to pedestrians on the crossing while the amber light is flashing. You must give pedestrians enough time to get to the other side of the road.

Perception

Seeing or noticing (as in Hazard Perception).

Peripheral vision

The area around the edges of your field of vision in which you can see movement but not details. Wearing a motorcycle helmet diminishes a motorcyclist's peripheral vision and means that riders need to use extremely careful observation while riding.

Positive attitude

Being sensible and obeying the law when you ride.

Priority

The vehicle or other road user that is allowed by law to go first is the one that has priority.

Protective clothing

Essential when riding, because it protects the rider from the weather, objects thrown up from the road or in case of an accident.

Provisional licence

A first motorcycle or car licence. All learners must get one before they start having lessons.

Puffin crossing

A type of pedestrian crossing that does not have a flashing amber light phase.

Reaction time

The amount of time it takes you to see a hazard and decide what to do about it.

Red route

You see these in London and some other cities. Double red lines at the edge of the road tell you that you must not stop or park there at any time. Single red lines have notices with times when you must not stop or park. Some red routes have marked bays for either parking or loading at certain times.

Residential areas

Areas of housing where people live. The speed limit is 30mph or sometimes 20mph.

Road hump

A low bump built across the road to slow vehicles down. Also called 'sleeping policemen'.

Road surface

The type and quality of the road that you are riding on. Slippery road surfaces, such as loose chippings, leaves and, even road markings, can make the road surface hazardous for riders, particularly in wet weather.

Rumble strips
Raised strips across the road near a roundabout or junction that change the sound the tyres make on the road surface, warning riders to slow down. They are also used on motorways to separate the main carriageway from the hard shoulder.

Safety margin
The amount of space you need to leave between your motorcycle and the vehicle in front so that you are not in danger of crashing into it if the driver slows down suddenly or stops. Safety margins have to be longer in wet or icy conditions.

Separation distance
The amount of space you need to leave between your motorcycle and the vehicle in front so that you are not in danger of crashing into it if the driver slows down suddenly or stops. The separation distance must be longer in wet or icy conditions.

Shoulder check
A term often used instead of 'lifesaver'.

Side stand
A metal support that enables you to stand your motorcycle when you want, for example, leave it parked. Leaving the side stand down when riding is extremely dangerous and could cause you to have a serious accident, particularly when cornering.

Single carriageway
Generally, a road with one lane in each direction.

Skid
When the tyres fail to grip the surface of the road, the subsequent loss of control of the motorcycle's movement is called a skid. Usually caused by harsh or fierce braking, steering or acceleration.

Slow-riding
Riding a motorcycle in a controlled manner at a walking pace using the throttle, clutch and rear brake.

Snaking
Moving from side to side. This sometimes happens with trailers when they are being towed too fast, or they are not properly loaded.

Staggered junction
Where you drive across another road. Instead of going straight across, you have to go a bit to the right or left.

Steering
Control of the direction of the motorcycle. May be affected by road surface condition and the weather.

Sterile
Clean and free from bacteria.

Stopping distance
The time it takes for you to stop your motorcycle – made up of 'thinking distance' and 'braking distance'.

Tailgating
Riding too closely behind another vehicle – either to harass the driver in front or to help you see in thick fog.

Tax disc
The disc you display to show that you have taxed your vehicle (see Vehicle Excise Duty, below).

Thinking distance
The time it takes you to notice something and take the right action. You need to add thinking distance to your braking distance to make up your total stopping distance.

Third-party insurance
An insurance policy that insures you against any claim by passengers or other persons for damage or injury to their person or property.

Toucan crossing
A type of pedestrian crossing that does not have a flashing amber light phase, and cyclists are allowed to ride across.

Tow
To pull something behind your motorcycle, possibly a small trailer.

Traction Control System (TCS)
A safety system that is fitted to some motorcycles that helps prevent rear-wheel spin on slippery road surfaces.

Traffic-calming measures
Speed humps, chicanes and other devices placed in roads to slow traffic down.

Tram

A public transport vehicle which moves along the streets on fixed rails, usually electrically powered by overhead lines.

Tread depth

The depth of the grooves in a motorcycle's tyres that help them grip the road surface. The grooves must all be at least 1mm deep.

Turbulence

Strong movement of air. For example, when a large vehicle passes a much smaller one.

Two-second rule

In normal riding, the ideal minimum distance between you and the vehicle in front can be timed using the 'two-second' rule. As the vehicle in front passes a fixed object (such as a signpost), say to yourself 'Only a fool breaks the two second rule'. It takes two seconds to say it. If you have passed the same object before you finish, you are too close – pull back.

Tyre pressures

The amount of air which must be pumped into a tyre in order for it to be correctly inflated.

Vehicle Excise Duty

The tax you pay for your motorcycle so that you may drive it on public roads.

Vehicle Registration Document

A record of details about a vehicle and its owner.

Vehicle watch scheme

A system for identifying vehicles that may have been stolen.

Vulnerable

At risk of harm or injury.

Waiting restrictions

Times when you may not park or load your motorcycle in a particular area.

Wheel alignment

To ensure smooth rotation at all speeds, the wheels of your motorcycle need to be aligned correctly. Poor alignment can cause wheel wobble and make riding and, in particular, cornering dangerous.

Wheel spin

When the motorcycle's wheels spin round out of control with no grip on the road surface.

Zebra crossing

A pedestrian crossing without traffic lights. It has an orange light, and is marked by black and white stripes on the road. Riders must stop for pedestrians to cross.

Answers to Questions

ALERTNESS – SECTION 1

1 AE	2 B	3 B	4 D	5 A	6 C	7 B	8 C	9 D
10 A	11 D	12 C	13 A	14 C	15 D	16 A	17 B	18 C
19 C	20 C	21 D	22 D	23 C	24 BDF	25 C	26 D	27 C
28 C	29 C	30 C	31 B	32 B	33 A	34 A	35 C	36 D
37 D	38 C							

ATTITUDE – SECTION 2

39 B	40 D	41 C	42 B	43 C	44 BD	45 D	46 A	47 C
48 B	49 C	50 D	51 D	52 B	53 B	54 BCD	55 ABE	56 A
57 D	58 B	59 A	60 A	61 B	62 A	63 A	64 C	65 A
66 B	67 D	68 D	69 D	70 A	71 C			

SAFETY AND YOUR MOTORCYCLE – SECTION 3

72 D	73 C	74 A	75 A	76 B	77 B	78 C	79 D	80 C
81 A	82 B	83 A	84 ABC	85 B	86 D	87 ACD	88 AE	89 BE
90 C	91 D	92 A	93 D	94 A	95 B	96 D	97 B	98 D
99 A	100 B	101 B	102 BC	103 BCDE	104 AD	105 CD	106 C	107 D
108 C	109 A	110 A	111 C	112 D	113 B	114 A	115 C	116 D
117 A	118 C	119 D	120 C	121 D	122 B	123 C	124 C	125 B
126 C	127 D	128 A	129 A	130 A	131 D	132 B	133 B	134 AB
135 ABF	136 BEF	137 C	138 ACF	139 C	140 B	141 D	142 C	143 D
144 D	145 D	146 A	147 AE	148 D	149 B	150 D	151 D	152 A
153 B	154 A	155 B	156 C	157 D	158 A	159 B	160 C	161 D
162 A	163 B	164 A	165 A	166 B	167 B	168 B	169 D	170 AB

Answers to Questions – Section 16

171 C	172 B	173 D	174 B	175 A	176 A	177 C	178 BDE	179 D
180 BC	181 D	182 D	183 D	184 D	185 BD	186 BE	187 B	188 D
189 A	190 B	191 AB	192 A	193 ABDF	194 AB	195 C	196 D	197 D
198 D	199 A	200 C	201 A	202 CD	203 D	204 D	205 BC	206 B
207 D	208 D	209 C	210 C	211 A	212 B	213 B	214 C	215 B
216 C	217 A	218 A	219 D	220 ACD				

221 AD	222 D	223 D	224 ABC	225 B	226 ACE	227 D	228 AB	229 A
230 D	231 C	232 B	233 B	234 D	235 B	236 A	237 D	238 A
239 D	240 CD	241 B	242 C	243 A	244 D	245 ACE	246 D	247 C
248 C	249 C	250 D	251 B	252 B	253 A	254 A	255 A	256 C
257 C	258 CD	259 A	260 B	261 A	262 A	263 C	264 BF	265 B
266 AE	267 A	268 D	269 D	270 C	271 B	272 B	273 C	274 A
275 ABD	276 ACE							

277 D	278 ABC	279 A	280 A	281 A	282 A	283 D	284 B	285 AE
286 B	287 B	288 C	289 AD	290 C	291 D	292 D	293 C	294 C
295 B	296 D	297 D	298 D	299 B	300 C	301 D	302 A	303 D
304 D	305 B	306 D	307 B	308 D	309 D	310 C	311 AC	312 C
313 C	314 A	315 D	316 C	317 D	318 ABC	319 C	320 B	321 AC
322 ABD	323 B	324 D	325 A	326 A	327 D	328 D	329 A	330 A
331 C	332 C	333 C	334 D	335 D	336 B	337 A	338 C	339 D
340 C	341 C	342 A	343 D	344 D	345 A	346 A	347 D	348 A

OTHER TYPES OF VEHICLE – SECTION 7

349 C	350 AB	351 A	352 A	353 B	354 B	355 D	356 B	357 A
358 BC	359 B	360 D	361 A	362 A	363 C	364 B	365 D	366 D
367 D	368 A	369 A						

MOTORCYCLE HANDLING – SECTION 8

370 B	371 AD	372 C	373 D	374 AB	375 A	376 BDE	377 BE	378 A
379 CE	380 D	381 C	382 B	383 C	384 A	385 C	386 C	387 A
388 ABC	389 C	390 D	391 C	392 D	393 A	394 D	395 D	396 ABD
397 D	398 A	399 A	400 C	401 D	402 A	403 A	404 A	405 D
406 ACDE	407 B	408 B	409 ACE	410 A	411 CD	412 D	413 A	414 BDF
415 C	416 D	417 C	418 DE	419 B	420 C	421 C	422 D	423 D
424 C	425 B	426 D						

MOTORWAY RULES – SECTION 9

427 A	428 C	429 A	430 C	431 D	432 D	433 A	434 B	435 A
436 ADEF	437 ADEF	438 D	439 D	440 D	441 D	442 A	443 B	444 C
445 B	446 C	447 A	448 C	449 A	450 D	451 A	452 C	453 C
454 C	455 C	456 C	457 C	458 B	459 C	460 B	461 B	462 A
463 B	464 B	465 D	466 CDF	467 C	468 D	469 C	470 D	471 B
472 A	473 A	474 B	475 D	476 D	477 B	478 D	479 D	480 B
481 C	482 D	483 D	484 C	485 A	486 D	487 D		

RULES OF THE ROAD – SECTION 10

488 A	489 DE	490 ACF	491 B	492 C	493 B	494 D	495 D	496 D
497 ABC	498 D	499 B	500 A	501 C	502 C	503 D	504 B	505 A
506 C	507 D	508 ADF	509 AD	510 A	511 B	512 A	513 B	514 A
515 D	516 A	517 D	518 D	519 C	520 A	521 ACE	522 B	523 C
524 D	525 BD	526 B	527 A	528 D	529 C	530 A	531 B	532 CDE
533 B	534 AE	535 B	536 A	537 ABD	538 A	539 B	540 B	541 A
542 D	543 A	544 B	545 C					

Answers to Questions – Section 16

ROAD AND TRAFFIC SIGNS – SECTION 11

546	C	547	B	548	A	549	D	550	A	551	C	552	B	553	B
554	A	555	D	556	D	557	A	558	A	559	B	560	A	561	D
562	B	563	D	564	D	565	D	566	A	567	C	568	B	569	D
570	C	571	B	572	A	573	B	574	B	575	C	576	C	577	A
578	C	579	B	580	C	581	B	582	D	583	D	584	C	585	D
586	C	587	A	588	B	589	C	590	D	591	A	592	D	593	B
594	D	595	B	596	A	597	A	598	A	599	A	600	B	601	B
602	A	603	D	604	ACEF	605	C	606	A	607	A	608	C	609	D
610	B	611	C	612	B	613	B	614	B	615	B	616	D	617	A
618	C	619	A	620	C	621	D	622	A	623	C	624	B	625	D
626	A	627	B	628	B	629	C	630	C	631	A	632	A	633	C
634	D	635	C	636	C	637	B	638	A	639	C	640	D	641	C
642	B	643	A	644	A	645	C	646	BDF	647	A	648	C	649	C
650	B	651	B	652	A	653	C	654	A	655	B	656	A	657	B
658	D	659	D	660	B	661	A	662	D	663	C	664	D	665	C
666	B	667	C	668	C	669	A	670	B	671	B	672	D	673	B
674	B	675	A	676	D	677	A	678	B	679	B	680	D	681	C
682	B	683	A	684	B	685	B	686	C	687	A	688	B	689	A
690	A	691	C	692	C	693	A	694	B	695	C	696	B	697	A
698	C	699	D	700	B										

DOCUMENTS – SECTION 12

701	BDE	702	ADF	703	A	704	C	705	C	706	B	707	B	708	ABF
709	BCE	710	BD	711	D	712	C	713	B	714	C	715	B	716	A
717	C	718	C	719	ABE	720	BE	721	BCE	722	C	723	B	724	B
725	BE	726	C	727	A	728	A	729	C	730	C	731	B	732	C
733	D	734	B	735	A	736	D	737	D	738	C	739	C	740	ABD
741	A														

ACCIDENTS – SECTION 13

742	B	743	C	744	A	745	B	746	A	747	ABCE	748	ADE	749	B
750	D	751	A	752	A	753	BD	754	B	755	ABE	756	A	757	ACF
758	A	759	ABD	760	ACE	761	DEF	762	ABE	763	ACF	764	AE	765	ACDE
766	C	767	BC	768	A	769	B	770	B	771	BDE	772	C	773	D
774	CD	775	D	776	C	777	B	778	D	779	B	780	BDE	781	A
782	B	783	AB	784	A	785	A	786	B	787	B	788	D	789	C
790	C	791	B	792	B	793	B	794	D	795	B	796	B	797	D
798	B	799	D	800	B											

MOTORCYCLE LOADING – SECTION 14

801	A	802	AD	803	B	804	ABC	805	ACD	806	D	807	A	808	C
809	B	810	C	811	D	812	A	813	A	814	B	815	CD	816	C
817	A	818	D	819	C	820	A	821	B	822	D	823	C	824	D
825	B	826	C	827	B	828	B	829	AE	830	D	831	ADE	832	C
833	AD														